.NET 10 Revealed

Master the Latest Advancements in .NET

Kajetan Duszyński

Apress®

.NET 10 Revealed: Master the Latest Advancements in .NET

Kajetan Duszyński
Warsaw, Poland

ISBN-13 (pbk): 979-8-8688-1888-2
https://doi.org/10.1007/979-8-8688-1889-9
ISBN-13 (electronic): 979-8-8688-1889-9

Managing Director, Apress Media LLC: Welmoed Spahr
Acquisitions Editor: Ryan Byrnes
Editorial Assistant: Gryffin Winkler
Copy Editor: Kezia Endsley

Cover designed by eStudioCalamar

Distributed to the book trade worldwide by Springer Science+Business Media New York, 1 New York Plaza, Suite 4600, New York, NY 10004-1562, USA. Phone 1-800-SPRINGER, fax (201) 348-4505, e-mail orders-ny@ springer-sbm.com, or visit www.springeronline.com. Apress Media, LLC is a California LLC and the sole member (owner) is Springer Science + Business Media Finance Inc (SSBM Finance Inc). SSBM Finance Inc is a **Delaware** corporation.

For information on translations, please e-mail booktranslations@springernature.com; for reprint, paperback, or audio rights, please e-mail bookpermissions@springernature.com.

Apress titles may be purchased in bulk for academic, corporate, or promotional use. eBook versions and licenses are also available for most titles. For more information, reference our Print and eBook Bulk Sales web page at http://www.apress.com/bulk-sales.

Any source code or other supplementary material referenced by the author in this book is available to readers on GitHub. For more detailed information, please visit https://www.apress.com/gp/services/ source-code.

If disposing of this product, please recycle the paper

Table of Contents

About the Author ....**xv**

About the Technical Reviewer ....**xvii**

Chapter 1: Introduction **1**

A Personal Journey Through .NET 1

Why This Book? 1

How to Use This Book 2

    For Web Development Enthusiasts 2

    For Desktop and Mobile Developers 2

What Makes This Book Different 3

    Focused on Real-World Applications 3

    Beyond Basic Implementation 3

    Strategic Knowledge Building 3

What This Book Is Not 4

Using the Book's Code Examples 4

A Living Technology 5

Chapter 2: Introduction to .NET **7**

A Brief History of .NET 7

Evolution from .NET Framework to .NET 10 8

    Overview of the .NET Ecosystem 8

    Looking Forward 9

Chapter 3: The Journey of C#: A Developer's Perspective **11**

Introduction 11

    The Journey of C#: A Developer's Perspective 11

    C# 14: Continuing the Tradition 12

Looking Back, Moving Forward 12

Running C# Without a Project: The New *dotnet run* 13

Overview of File-Based C# Apps 13

Why Is This Useful? 14

Behind the Scenes... 15

Summary 15

File-Level Directives: Using *#:package, #:sdk,* and *#:property* for Standalone Files 15

Shebang Support and Scripting: Making C# Files Executable as Scripts on UNIX-like Systems 17

Major Language Changes in C# 14 19

Extension Members 19

The *field* Keyword for Auto-Properties 21

Null-Conditional Assignment 23

nameof with Unbound Generic Types 24

Lambda Parameter Modifiers 26

Practical Examples 27

First-Class *Span<T>* and *ReadOnlySpan<T>* Support................................. 29

Partial Events and Constructors 31

Recap of the Most Impactful C# 14 Changes 35

Chapter 4: Modern APIs with ASP.NET Core 10 37

Introduction.. 37

Minimal APIs vs. Controller-based APIs: When and Why................................ 38

Where Does .NET 10 Fit In? 38

About the Sample Application 39

Why Use a Task Management System?.. 39

Application Structure... 39

Design Principles 40

Using the Sample App 40

API-Wide Improvements in .NET 10 41

Integration Testing Enhancements 41

What's New in .NET 10? 41

Before .NET 10: The Workaround 42

After .NET 10: Seamless Integration 42

OpenAPI Updates 43

OpenAPI 3.1 Support 43

Customizing OpenAPI Output 45

Generating OpenAPI Documents in YAML Format 47

Enabling YAML Output 47

Current Limitations 47

General API Improvements 48

How Does It Work? 49

Minimal APIs Deep Dive 50

Validation Support in Minimal APIs 50

How Does It Work? 50

Enabling Validation 50

Advanced: Disabling Validation for Specific Endpoints 52

Custom Validation Logic 52

Treating Empty Strings as Null for Nullable Value Types in Form Posts 53

Authentication and Authorization 54

What's New in .NET 10: Metrics 54

Introducing and Measuring Auth Metrics 56

Chapter 5: Blazor in .NET 10: Modern Web UI, Productivity, and Experience 59

Introduction 59

Blazor in .NET 10: A Quick Overview 60

Performance and Resource Optimizations 61

Blazor Script as a static Web Asset 61

WebAssembly Runtime Diagnostics 63

UI and Component Enhancements 66

QuickGrid Improvements in .NET 10 66

Reconnection UI Updates 71

Declarative State Persistence 75

Navigation and Routing Improvements 79

NavigateTo Behavior Changes: No More Scroll Jumps 80

Route Template Highlighting in Code Editors 80

Enhanced *NavLink* Matching 81

Improved Handling of "Not Found" Pages with the *NotFound* Method 82

Security and Authentication Updates 83

The Old Way: .NET 9 and Its Challenges 83

The New Way: .NET 10 Makes It Simple and Scalable 84

Distributed Token Cache: Ready for the Real World 85

OpenID Connect and Windows Auth Considerations 86

Why This Matters 86

Interactivity and Real-Time Features 86

Native Support for Server-Sent Events (SSE) 86

How SSE Compares to SignalR 88

Migration and Compatibility Considerations 89

Serving Blazor Scripts as Static Assets: Migration Considerations 89

AppContext Switches for Legacy Navigation Behavior 90

Breaking Changes and How to Address Them 90

Making the Most of .NET 10 91

Best Practices and Real-World Scenarios 91

Tips for Leveraging New Blazor Features in Production 92

Sample Use Cases: Dashboards, Admin Panels, and Real-Time Apps 92

Common Pitfalls and How to Avoid Them 93

Bringing It All Together 93

Chapter 6: Unlocking .NET MAUI's Potential **95**

Introduction 95

Getting Started with .NET MAUI in .NET 10 96

Setting Up a New MAUI Project Targeting .NET 10 96

Upgrading Existing MAUI Projects 97

.NET MAUI Workload and NuGet Package Updates 98

Best Practices 98

XAML Improvements and Simplification in .NET MAUI 10 99

Global and Implicit XML Namespaces in XAML 99

Cleaner XAML Files: Removing Boilerplate Code 100

Adopting New XAML Features in Existing Projects 100

.NET Aspire Integration 101

What Is .NET Aspire and Why It Matters for MAUI 101

Using the New .NET Aspire Project Template 102

Telemetry, Service Discovery, and Configuration for Mobile Apps 103

Control Enhancements and Deprecations 103

CollectionView and CarouselView 104

Entry and Editor: Android Feels Native 107

HybridWebView: New Ways to Interact with Web Content 108

New Capabilities of Switch and SearchBar 108

Deprecated Controls and Migration 109

Animation API Modernization 113

The Move to Async Animation Methods 113

Practical Usage and Migration Tips 113

Platform-Specific Features and Updates 114

iOS and Mac Catalyst 115

Android 116

Cross-Platform Improvements 119

Modernizing Media and File Pickers 123

MediaPicker Improvements: Resize, Compress, and EXIF Support 123

Nullable DatePicker and TimePicker Controls 125

Performance and Quality Improvements 126

Overview of Performance Boosts and Bug Fixes 126

Impact on App Startup, Rendering, and Memory Usage 127

Summary and Next Steps 128

Recap of the Most Important Changes 128

Recommendations for Developers New to MAUI or .NET 10 129

Chapter 7: Performance and Optimization 131

Introduction 131

    Why Performance Matters in Modern Apps 131

    Key Themes in .NET 10: Reducing Abstraction, Lowering Memory Usage, and Generating Smarter Code 132

    What to Expect in this Chapter 132

The .NET 10 Optimization Philosophy 133

    Focusing on Real-World Developer Scenarios 133

    Balancing Runtime Speed, Memory Efficiency, and Code Simplicity 133

    Continuous Journey from .NET Core to Latest Release 133

JIT Compiler Enhancements 134

    Improved Layout of Method Code Blocks for Better CPU Caching and Pipelining ... 134

    Loop Inversion and Optimizations for Common Loops 134

Devirtualization and Inlining Improvements 137

    Array Interface Method Devirtualization 137

    Inlining of Late Devirtualized Methods 138

    Devirtualization Based on Inlining Observations 138

Escape Analysis and Stack Allocation 139

    Escape Analysis for Better Lifetime Management 139

    Stack Allocation for Small Arrays of Value Types and Reference Types 139

Array Enumeration Deabstraction 141

    Direct Array Iteration vs. *IEnumerable* Penalties 141

    Reduction of Cost When Using Abstraction in Code 141

Stack Allocation of Arrays 142

    When and How Value-Type and Reference-Type Arrays Are Stack-Allocated ... 142

    Value-Type Arrays 143

    Reference-Type Arrays 143

    GC Pressure Reduction and Application Startup Speed 144

    Practical Takeaways 145

Region-Based GC Information 145

    New APIs for Introspection: *GC.GetMemoryInfo* Improvements 145

    Using Region Info to Troubleshoot Memory Fragmentation 146

Improved Arm64 Write-Barriers 147

    Details on Better Collection Performance on Arm64 Systems 147

    Default Write-Barrier Changes and Their Effect on Pause Times 147

Thread Pool Metrics and Monitoring 148

    New APIs to Monitor Thread Pool Health and Behavior 148

    Optimizing for High-Throughput, Scalable Applications 149

    Best Practices 150

Real-World Parallelism Tweaks 150

    Updates to Library Concurrency Primitives 150

    Practical Guidance for Developers 151

SIMD and Vectorization Improvements 153

    AVX10.2 and SIMD Enhancements 153

    Impact on Numerical Computing and Image Processing Workloads 153

Enhanced Metrics APIs 155

    GC Insights 155

    Thread Pool Insights 155

    Method Tiering Insights 156

    Gathering Actionable Metrics During Execution 156

Chapter 8: EF Core and .NET Libraries 157

Introduction 157

    Demystifying .NET Libraries and EF Core 157

    Staying Current: Why It Really Matters 157

    The Big Picture with .NET 10 158

Entity Framework Core 10: Major New Features and Enhancements 158

    Discovering *LeftJoin* and *RightJoin* 159

    Simpler LINQ Translations 160

    Expanded Operator Support: *GroupBy* and Aggregates with Clean SQL 160

ExecuteUpdateAsync Improvements in EF Core 10 161

    A More Flexible Pattern for Bulk Updates 161

    Expression vs. Non-Expression Lambda Parameter Support 162

    Practical Benefits 163

Enhanced Azure Cosmos DB Integration in EF Core 10 163

    Unlocking Powerful Search: Full-Text Capabilities 164

    Smarter Discovery: Hybrid and Vector Similarity Search with RRF 164

    Growing Without Pain: Effortless Model Evolution and Default Values 165

General Query and Performance Enhancements in EF Core 10 167

    Smarter Query Translation for *DateOnly* and *TimeOnly* 167

    Optimized Handling of Limit and Count Operations 167

    Support for String Functions with *char* Arguments 168

    Performance Improvements for *MIN*, *MAX*, and *DISTINCT* 169

Usability and API Updates in EF Core 10 169

    Simplified Naming for Generated SQL Query Parameters 170

    New Features for Logging and Sensitive Data Redaction 170

    Updates to Model Configuration Patterns 171

Advanced Performance and Compiled Models in EF Core 10 172

    Compiling EF Core Models for Faster Startup 172

    Using the *dbcontext optimize* Tooling 173

    Why These Performance Gains Matter 173

Core .NET 10 Libraries: What's New Across the Board 174

    ISOWeek Now Supports *DateOnly*: Precision for Week-Based Calculations 174

    String Normalization for Spans: Faster Text Processing, Fewer Allocations 174

    Numeric Ordering for String Comparison: Sorting That Makes Sense 175

    More Expressive Overloads for *OrderedDictionary* and *DateTime* 175

    Updates to *TimeSpan.FromMilliseconds* 176

    Enhancements for Matrix Transformation Methods 176

Performance and Memory Improvements in .NET 10 177

    ZipArchive: Faster, Leaner File Compression and Extraction 177

    Stack Allocation for Small Arrays: Lightning Fast, Zero Garbage 178

Array Interface and Enumeration Optimizations: Minimal Abstraction, Maximal Speed...... 178

Diagnostics, Observability, and Telemetry in .NET 10 179

Telemetry Schema URL Support in ActivitySource and Meter 179

Updates to Match OpenTelemetry Specifications 180

Chapter 9: Migration and Compatibility 181

Introduction 181

Why Migration Matters in .NET 10 181

The Importance of Compatibility 182

Key Migration and Compatibility Goals in .NET 10 182

Understanding .NET 10: Overview for Migration 182

What's New in .NET 10 for Migration 183

LTS and Support Lifecycle 183

Supported Platforms and System Requirements 184

Planning Your Migration 184

Inventory and Assessment of Existing Applications 184

Choosing a Migration Strategy 185

Breaking Changes in .NET 10 186

How Breaking Changes Are Documented and Categorized 187

Migration from .NET Framework, .NET Core, and .NET 5–9 188

Differences Between .NET Framework and .NET 10 189

Key Benefits of Migrating from Older .NET Versions 189

Special Considerations for Legacy Technologies... 189

Modernizing Architecture: Monolith to Microservices 190

Updating Project Files and Dependencies 191

Moving to SDK-Style Projects... 191

Target Framework Monikers (TFM) for .NET 10... 191

Upgrading NuGet Packages and Third-Party Dependencies... 192

Dealing with Deprecated APIs 192

Migrating ASP.NET Applications 192

Changes in the ASP.NET API Surface 193

Updated Project Structure and Hosting Model 193

OpenAPI 3.1 and Other Web API Changes 193

Migration of Middleware and Routing 194

Migrating Blazor, MAUI, and Other UI Technologies 194

Libraries, Packages, and Third-Party Integrations 196

Ensuring Third-Party Compatibility (NuGet, DLLs) 196

Upgrading Data Access Patterns (EF Core, Dapper) 196

Globalization, Serialization, and Cryptography Updates 197

Containers and Cloud Readiness 198

Changes in Default Images and Container Support 198

Cloud-Native Migration (Docker, Kubernetes Integration) 198

Deploying and Testing .NET 10 in Containers 199

Testing, Validation, and Quality Assurance 200

Side-by-Side Testing and Functional Verification 200

Using Profilers, Linters, and Compatibility Analyzers 201

Performance Profiling Tools in .NET 10 201

Pitfalls, Troubleshooting, and Best Practices 202

Common Migration Pitfalls 202

How to Diagnose and Fix Compatibility Issues 203

Rollback and Contingency Strategies 203

Keeping DevOps Pipelines Compatible 204

Conclusion and Next Steps 204

Staying Up to Date with .NET Releases 204

Continuing Education and Resources for .NET 10 Migrators 205

Encouragement for a Smooth Transition 206

Chapter 10: The Future of .NET 207

Introduction: The Significance of .NET's Future 207

The Evolving .NET Ecosystem 208

Unified Platform Vision 208

The Function of Blazor, MAUI, and Other Frameworks for .NET 208

Community and Open-Source Growth 209

    How the Community Shapes .NET's Roadmap 209

    The Importance of Open Standards and Cross-Community Partnerships 210

    Why This Matters for the Future 210

Advances in JIT and Native AOT 211

    Just-In-Time (JIT) Compilation Improvements in .NET 8–10 211

    Native Ahead-of-Time (AOT) Compilation: Impact on Startup, Memory, and Deployment ... 212

    Practical Impact 212

Lower-Level Optimizations in .NET 10 213

Memory and Garbage Collection Innovations 214

Security and Reliability in a Changing World 215

    Evolving Authentication, Authorization, and Cryptography 215

    Proactive Adaptation to New Security Threats 216

Resilient Cloud and Distributed Systems 216

    Built-In Support for Cloud-Native Patterns 216

    High Availability, Failover, and Telemetry Advances 217

Modern Application Development Toolkit 218

    API Design and Minimalism 218

Cross-Platform User Experience 219

    The Evolution of .NET MAUI 219

    Blazor Advancements for Device-Consistent UIs 219

Enhancements in Tooling and Productivity 220

    Smarter CLI 220

    IDE Experience: Visual Studio, VS Code, and Rider 221

    Testing Workflows 221

    Code Analysis and Refactoring 221

    AI-Assisted Development 222

What You Can Expect Beyond .NET 10 222

Conclusion: Preparing for the Future with .NET 224

Index 227

About the Author

Kajetan Duszyński is a Microsoft MVP with over a decade of experience as a software engineer. He is the founder of the DotNet School in Poland and regularly speaks at .NET conferences. Kajetan creates tutorials and courses about .NET and keeps an audience of many thousands informed through his newsletter, podcast, YouTube channel, and various social media communities.

About the Technical Reviewer

 **Mahendran Chinnaiah** is a seasoned and visionary digital healthcare architect with over 18 years of experience delivering transformative enterprise solutions across the healthcare continuum. He holds various technical certifications, including those from Microsoft (MCTS), cloud platforms such as Azure and Google Cloud, and big data technologies like Cloudera. His work bridges technology, clinical operations, PBM, insurance, and policy compliance, consistently driving innovation, efficiency, and measurable impact.

Introduction

I still remember 2012 when I started my first job as a C#/.NET developer. I opened Visual Studio to work on a Silverlight project. Fresh out of university and having some theoretical knowledge but little practical experience, I started diving into the world of .NET Framework 4. Little did I know that this was the beginning of a 13-year journey that influenced my entire career.

A Personal Journey Through .NET

The .NET ecosystem has evolved dramatically since those days. I've witnessed the transformation from the monolithic .NET Framework to the cross-platform revolution of .NET Core, and now to the unified .NET platform we have today. As a Microsoft MVP and someone who has lived through these changes, I've seen technologies come and go, patterns evolve, and development practices transform.

This book is more than just a technical guide—it's a culmination of lessons learned and insights gained from working with .NET across its many iterations. From building enterprise applications to mentoring junior developers, I've experienced first-hand the power and versatility of this platform.

Why This Book?

We all have the same problem. Current .NET release roadmap is so intense that it's hard to keep up with rapid pace of evolution. Every year we witness a huge list of changes in absolutely every field of .NET. The Internet is filled with *Top 10 changes from .NET X that you need to implement right now!* kind of videos and blog posts. These different approaches are not making it easy to find a coherent narrative about what's new and actually important, especially for beginners.

© Kajetan Duszyński 2025
K. Duszyński, *.NET 10 Revealed*, https://doi.org/10.1007/979-8-8688-1889-9_1

I've created this book to close this gap. It's the guide I wish I had when I was starting out, back when books were the best source of info. It's combined with the latest innovations in .NET 10, delivered in an easy way to consume so you can implement your own projects.

How to Use This Book

One of the beautiful aspects of modern .NET development is its modularity—you don't need to know everything to be productive. This book attempts to reflect that philosophy. That's why, depending on your area of expertise, you can choose one of the paths outline here.

For Web Development Enthusiasts

- Begin with Chapters 3-5, which cover C# in general, Blazor, and minimal APIs.

- These chapters reflect the evolution from traditional web development to modern, lightweight approaches.

- Essential companion chapters: Chapters 7-10 for crucial cross-cutting concerns.

For Desktop and Mobile Developers

- Check out Chapter 3, which covers C# in general.

- Chapter 6 on .NET MAUI is your starting point.

- As the natural evolution of Xamarin, .NET MAUI brings cross-platform development to a new level, allowing you to build desktop and mobile applications from a single codebase.

- Chapters 7-10 provide critical knowledge for building robust applications.

Remember, modern .NET development is all about picking the right tools for your specific needs. Once you grasp the basics in the first two chapters, you'll be well-equipped to dive into any other part of the book that interests you.

What Makes This Book Different

This book stands apart by focusing on what matters most: your growth and success as a .NET developer. While other resources might overwhelm you with exhaustive technical details, this book cuts through the complexity to deliver practical, actionable knowledge.

Focused on Real-World Applications

Each concept and feature is presented through the lens of practical application.

Within each chapter, you will create applications that show how to use .NET 10 features to solve actual development challenges. When exploring new performance improvements, for instance, you'll see exactly how they can enhance your applications and when to best utilize them. The book does not have time and space to show every bit of code, but if you want, you can jump on GitHub at any time to access full apps with all the features.

Beyond Basic Implementation

While official documentation tells you what features exist, this book shows you how to use them effectively. You'll learn about:

- The context behind new features and when to use them

- Performance implications of different implementation choices

Strategic Knowledge Building

The book is structured to help you build knowledge strategically. Instead of overwhelming you with everything at once, each chapter is continuation of previous ones. You will build apps based on what you already know. Each chapter is also self-contained enough to serve as a reference. This approach allows you to:

- Quickly identify which features are relevant to your projects

- Understand the impact of new .NET 10 capabilities on your development workflow

- Make informed decisions about adopting new technologies

This book aims to be your practical guide through .NET 10, helping you make best decisions and implement solutions effectively. Whether you're building web applications, desktop software, or mobile apps, you'll find the knowledge you need to use .NET 10's capabilities and utilize its potential.

What This Book Is Not

In the interest of transparency, let me be clear about what this book doesn't cover:

- It's not an exhaustive guide to all things.NET

- It doesn't dive deep into basic programming concepts

- It's not a replacement for official documentation

Instead, it focuses on what's new in .NET 10, explained in a way that beginners and experienced developers can both appreciate.

Using the Book's Code Examples

All code examples presented in this book are available in the GitHub repository. Whether you're following along with the evolution of .NET from Chapter 2 or experimenting with the latest C# 14 features, you won't need to manually type the code samples.

Each chapter has its own directory in the repository, organized by topics and sections. The code is structured to match the book's progression, making it easy to find specific examples. For instance, when you explore new C# 14 features in Chapter 3, you'll find complete, working examples ready to run in your development environment.

While having access to the code is convenient, I encourage you to experiment with it. Modify the examples, break them, and rebuild them. There's no better way to learn than by getting your hands dirty with actual code. Think of these examples as a starting point for your own exploration of .NET 10's capabilities.

A Living Technology

As someone who started with Silverlight (rest in peace) and witnessed the rise of technologies like ASP.NET Core and Blazor, I can tell you that .NET is constantly evolving. This book captures the current state of .NET 10 while preparing you for future changes.

Whether you're starting your journey in software development or looking to stay current with the latest in .NET, this book is designed to be your practical guide. Feel free to jump between chapters based on your interests and needs—after all, that's how modern development works.

Let's begin this journey together, exploring what .NET 10 has to offer and how it can help you build better software. But first... let's start with some introduction to .NET itself.

CHAPTER 2

Introduction to .NET

Software development is all about constant evolution and the .NET story is (from my perspective) one of the most fascinating in the tech world. From its beginnings as a Windows-only framework to today's powerful cross-platform ecosystem, .NET has changed our thinking about how software should be built. Let's explore this journey together.

A Brief History of .NET

In the late 1990s, Microsoft faced a challenge: how to make Windows development more accessible and powerful while keeping up with the Internet revolution. Their answer was .NET, launched in 2002 as .NET Framework 1.0. This first version introduced two concepts: the Common Language Runtime (CLR), which managed how programs ran, and a unified way to build web applications with ASP.NET.

Think of the CLR as a universal translator—it allowed developers to write code in different languages like C# or Visual Basic, and it ensured that everything worked together smoothly. This was quite a change at the time, as previously, each programming language needed its own separate system.

The early years saw rapid growth. Version 2.0 brought features we now take for granted, like generic collections. Imagine being able to create a list that could specifically hold only numbers or only text, making the code safer and more efficient. Version 3.0 introduced Windows Presentation Foundation (WPF), revolutionizing how developers built desktop applications with its graphics and animation capabilities.

© Kajetan Duszyński 2025
K. Duszyński, *.NET 10 Revealed*, https://doi.org/10.1007/979-8-8688-1889-9_2

Evolution from .NET Framework to .NET 10

Microsoft and .NET devs lived with the conviction that there wasn't any other OS than Windows for many years. We were happy to deliver our apps to Windows and Windows only. The real transformation began when Microsoft realized that the future of software wasn't just about Windows. The world was changing—smartphones were everywhere, Linux was growing in popularity, and cloud computing was becoming essential. The original .NET Framework, while powerful, was like a mighty oak tree—strong but firmly rooted in Windows soil.

.NET Core was introduced in 2016. It wasn't anything like we knew before. It wasn't just an update; it was a complete reimagining. Microsoft took the bold step of making .NET open-source and cross-platform. Suddenly, developers could build applications that ran on Windows, Linux, and macOS using the same code (or at least that was the plan). It was like giving that mighty oak tree wings.

The journey continued with each new version bringing significant improvements. .NET 5 in 2020 marked another moment of big change—Microsoft dropped the "Core" name, unifying different .NET implementations into a single platform. This meant that developers no longer needed to choose between different versions of .NET for different types of applications.

.NET 6 and 7 focused on making development faster and more efficient. .NET 8 brought native AOT compilation, allowing applications to start almost instantly, while .NET 9 embraced AI integration.

Overview of the .NET Ecosystem

Today's .NET is a great ecosystem where all pieces can be integrated within each other almost seamlessly. There is still the runtime environment as a beating heart of each app, managing memory and executing code efficiently. Around it, you'll find tools and frameworks for every kind of application you might want to build.

Want to create web applications? ASP.NET Core and Blazor offer modern, efficient way to build everything from simple websites to complex web applications. Need to develop desktop software? Windows Forms, WPF, and .NET MAUI provide options for different needs. Mobile development? .NET MAUI lets you build iOS and Android apps from the same codebase.

The ecosystem extends beyond just frameworks. Libraries that are created within .NET gives plenty of possibilities. Entity Framework Core simplifies database operations, making it feel almost like working with regular objects. SignalR enables real-time communication in applications, perfect for chat applications or live updates. And with ML.NET, you can integrate machine learning capabilities into your applications without being a data science expert.

What makes this ecosystem truly special is how naturally these pieces work together. You can build a web API using minimal APIs, create a mobile app with .NET MAUI that consumes this API, and deploy everything to the cloud with Azure, all while sharing code and using the same development tools.

Looking Forward

As we stand at the threshold of .NET 10, it's clear that the platform has come a long way from its Windows-only roots. Today's .NET is open-source, cross-platform, and community-driven, yet it maintains the reliability and performance that made it popular in the first place.

The coming chapters explore what .NET 10 brings to this rich ecosystem. Whether you're building web applications, mobile apps, or desktop software, you'll discover how the latest features and improvements can help you create better software more efficiently.

Remember, while .NET's capabilities are huge, you don't need to master everything at once. Start with what's relevant to your current needs and let your knowledge grow naturally as you explore more of what this platform has to offer.

CHAPTER 3

The Journey of C#: A Developer's Perspective

Introduction

C# is a language that has grown up alongside many of us. If you've been developing with C# for over 15 years, you've witnessed a remarkable transformation—from a statically typed, object-oriented language to a modern, expressive, and developer-friendly tool that keeps getting better with every release. C# 14 continues this tradition, focusing on making your daily coding more productive, approachable, and enjoyable.

The Journey of C#: A Developer's Perspective

When C# 2.0 arrived in 2005, it brought generics, partial classes, and nullable types, making it easier to write reusable and type-safe code. Generics, for example, let you write a `List<T>` instead of creating separate collections for every data type—a game changer for code reuse and safety. Partial classes allowed teams to split class definitions across files, making collaborative work much smoother.

A couple of years later, C# 3.0 introduced features like LINQ, lambda expressions, and extension methods. LINQ made querying data collections as easy as writing SQL, and lambda expressions brought a functional flavor to C#, letting you write concise, readable code. Extension methods let you add new capabilities to existing types, which made code organization and readability so much better.

With C# 5.0, asynchronous programming became mainstream. The introduction of `async` and `await` made it possible to write non-blocking code that looked just like synchronous code, greatly simplifying tasks like web requests and file I/O. This was a huge leap for building responsive applications.

C# 6.0 and 7.x kept the momentum going with features like string interpolation, null propagation, pattern matching, tuples, local functions, and more. These additions steadily reduced boilerplate code and made code more expressive and easier to maintain.

More recently, C# 8.0 and beyond introduced nullable reference types, default interface methods, and improved pattern matching, all aimed at making code safer and more robust. At each step along the way, C# has listened to its developer community and evolved to fit real-world needs.

C# 14: Continuing the Tradition

C# 14 is all about making development even smoother. The focus is on features that cut down on repetitive code, boost performance, and let you focus on solving problems instead of wrestling with syntax. For example, the new `field` keyword for auto-properties lets you add logic to property getters and setters without having to declare explicit backing fields, reducing clutter and making your intent clearer.

Another standout is the improved support for `Span<T>` and `ReadOnlySpan<T>`, which allows for high-performance memory access with less boilerplate code. Implicit conversions between arrays and spans mean you can write more efficient code without sacrificing readability.

The language also introduces more flexibility in lambda expressions, allowing you to use modifiers like `ref`, `in`, and `out` directly in parameter lists—no need to specify types every time. This makes functional-style programming in C# more powerful and approachable.

And perhaps the most exciting change for many developers: you can now run a single `.cs` file directly using the `dotnet run` command, without creating a full project. This makes C# as easy to try out as scripting languages like Python or JavaScript, lowering the barrier for experimentation, learning, and quick prototyping.

Looking Back, Moving Forward

If you've been coding in C# since the early days, you've seen it transform from a language that required lots of ceremony to one that's modern, concise, and developer-centric. Each new version has introduced features that made the job easier, the code cleaner, and the applications more robust.

C# 14 continues this journey, focusing on what matters most: letting you write great software with less effort. Whether you're just starting out or have been coding in C# for decades, these improvements are designed to help you be more productive and creative every day.

The following sections dive into the latest features of C# 14, showing how they build on the language's rich history and how you can use them to write better code right now.

Running C# Without a Project: The New *dotnet run*

C# 14 introduces a major improvement for developers: you can now run C# code directly from a single `.cs` file, without having to set up a full project. This makes C# feel lighter, faster, and more approachable, especially for quick experiments, learning, or automation tasks.

Overview of File-Based C# Apps

Traditionally, running C# code required creating a project structure with a `.csproj` file, even for the simplest programs. With .NET 10, you can skip all of that and run a `.cs` file directly using the command line.

How It Works

- **Create a C# file:** Write your code in a file, for example `hello.cs`.

- **Run it instantly:** Use the `dotnet run hello.cs` command.

The .NET CLI will compile and execute your file on the spot—no project setup needed.

Example

Suppose you have a file named `hello.cs` with the following code:

```
Console.WriteLine("Hello from a project-less world in .NET 10!");
```

To run it, open your terminal, navigate to the file's folder, and type the following:

```
dotnet run hello.cs
```

Expected Output

```
Hello from a project-less world in .NET 10!
```

This immediate feedback makes it easy to test ideas, teach concepts, and automate small tasks without any extra setup.

Why Is This Useful?

The ability to run a C# file directly with `dotnet run` brings a new level of simplicity and flexibility to the language, making it much more approachable in a wide range of scenarios. For many years, C# was seen as a language that required a lot of setup, with every new idea and experiment needing a full project structure and configuration files. Now, with file-based apps, that barrier has disappeared, and developers can jump straight into coding without any ceremony.

This new approach is especially valuable for those who want to experiment with ideas, write quick scripts, or learn the language without being overwhelmed by project scaffolding. Imagine wanting to test a small piece of logic or automate a simple task—previously, you would have needed to create a new project, configure it, and only then write your code. With C# 14 and .NET 10, you simply create a `.cs` file, write your code, and run it instantly. This makes C# feel as lightweight and immediate as scripting languages like Python, while still providing all the power and safety of the .NET ecosystem.

Another significant advantage is that this feature lowers the entry barrier for new developers. Beginners can focus on learning the language and seeing results right away, rather than getting bogged down by project setup. This immediacy encourages experimentation and learning, making C# a more attractive choice for those just starting out in programming.

For experienced developers, the ability to quickly prototype or share code snippets becomes much easier. Sharing a single file is straightforward, and there's no need to worry about missing project files or dependencies. Plus, when a script grows in complexity and needs to become a full application, converting it into a standard project is seamless and doesn't require rewriting or restructuring your code.

Finally, this approach ensures consistency across the development experience. The same language, runtime, and tooling are used for both file-based and project-based apps, so moving from a simple script to a robust application is smooth and intuitive. This unified workflow supports everything from quick one-off scripts to large-scale software projects, all within the same ecosystem.

Behind the Scenes

When you run a `.cs` file this way, .NET creates a virtual project in memory, compiles your code, and executes it. If your script grows and you want to convert it into a full project, you can use this:

```
dotnet project convert hello.cs
```

This command creates a new project structure and migrates your code, making it easy to scale up when needed.

Summary

Running C# files directly with `dotnet run` brings the convenience of scripting languages to the C# world, while keeping all the power and safety of the .NET ecosystem. It's a big step forward for productivity and approachability, making C# more accessible than ever before.

File-Level Directives: Using *#:package, #:sdk*, and *#:property* for Standalone Files

With C# 14 and .NET 10, you can now add special file-level directives at the top of your standalone `.cs` files to configure dependencies, SDKs, and build properties, all without needing a project file. These directives make your scripts more powerful and flexible, letting you pull in libraries, set up your runtime environment, and tweak compilation settings right where your code lives.

What Are File-Level Directives?

File-level directives begin with `#:` and must appear before any code in your `.cs` file. There are three main types:

- `#:package` for referencing NuGet packages

- `#:sdk` for specifying the SDK

- `#:property` for setting build properties

These directives are only recognized in file-based C# apps and are ignored in traditional project-based applications.

Adding NuGet Packages with *#:package*

Suppose you want to use the `Newtonsoft.Json` package to serialize an object to JSON. You can add the following at the top of your script:

```
#:package Newtonsoft.Json@13.0.3

using Newtonsoft.Json;

var person = new { Name = "Alex", Age = 34 };
string json = JsonConvert.SerializeObject(person);
Console.WriteLine(json);
```

When you run this file with `dotnet run file.cs`, the CLI will automatically download the package and make it available to your code.

You can also use less common packages. For example, if you want to generate QR codes in your script, you use this:

```
#:package QRCoder@1.4.3

using QRCoder;

QRCodeGenerator qrGenerator = new QRCodeGenerator();
QRCodeData qrCodeData = qrGenerator.CreateQrCode("https://dotnet.microsoft.
                        com", QRCodeGenerator.ECCLevel.Q);
AsciiQRCode qrCode = new AsciiQRCode(qrCodeData);
string qrCodeAsAsciiArt = qrCode.GetGraphic(1);
Console.WriteLine(qrCodeAsAsciiArt);
```

This lets you create and display a QR code directly from a standalone script, without setting up a project.

Choosing an SDK with *#:sdk*

If you want to create a simple Windows Forms application as a script, you can specify the required SDK:

```
#:sdk Microsoft.NET.Sdk.WindowsDesktop
#:property UseWindowsForms true

using System.Windows.Forms;

Application.Run(new Form { Text = "Hello from WinForms Script!" });
```

This allows you to launch a Windows Forms window just by running your `.cs` file, something that previously required a full project setup.

Setting Build Properties with *#:property*

You might want to enable nullable reference types and set a specific language version for your script. You can do this with the following directives:

```
#:property Nullable enable
#:property LangVersion 14.0
```

For example, you can write a script that checks for null values and leverages the latest language features:

```
#:property Nullable enable
#:property LangVersion 14.0

string? name = null;
Console.WriteLine(name?.ToUpper() ?? "No name provided.");
```

You can also set properties that are more advanced, like enabling trimming for smaller output binaries:

```
#:property PublishTrimmed true
```

This is useful if you're writing a script that you plan to publish as a small, self-contained tool.

How to Use Directives

Always place each directive on its own line at the very top of your `.cs` file, before any code. You can use multiple `#:package` and `#:property` directives, but only one `#:sdk` directive per file. When you run your script, the .NET CLI will process these directives, download any packages, and apply the specified settings automatically.

Shebang Support and Scripting: Making C# Files Executable as Scripts on UNIX-like Systems

One of the most exciting additions in C# 14 and .NET 10 is full support for shebang lines, making it possible to use C# files as first-class scripts on UNIX-like systems such as Linux and macOS. This brings C# closer to scripting languages like Python or Bash, allowing you to write and run scripts directly from the terminal with minimal setup.

What Is a Shebang Line?

A *shebang* (#!) is a special line at the very top of a script file that tells the operating system which interpreter should be used to execute the script. For C#, this means you can specify that your script should be run using the dotnet run command, enabling direct execution from the shell.

How to Use Shebang in C# Scripts

To make a C# file executable as a script, add the following line as the first line in your .cs file:

```
#!/usr/bin/env dotnet run
```

This line tells the operating system to use the dotnet run command to interpret and execute your file. After adding the shebang, you need to make your file executable by running:

```
chmod +x yourscript.cs
```

Now, you can run your C# script just like any other shell script:

```
./yourscript.cs
```

The script will execute, and you'll see the output in your terminal, just as if you had run it with dotnet run yourscript.cs.

Example

Suppose you have a script called greet.cs:

```
#!/usr/bin/env dotnet run

Console.WriteLine("Hello from a C# script!");
```

After making it executable, running ./greet.cs will print the following:

```
Hello from a C# script!
```

This makes it incredibly easy to write automation scripts, quick utilities, or even teaching examples without any project setup.

Major Language Changes in C# 14

C# 14 introduces a set of new features that make the language more expressive, powerful, and enjoyable for developers of all skill levels. These changes are designed to help you write cleaner code, reduce boilerplate code, and unlock new programming patterns that were previously difficult or impossible in earlier versions of C#. This section explores the most significant updates, starting with one of the headline features: extension members.

Extension Members

Extension members are a major enhancement in C# 14, building on the familiar concept of extension methods. Previously, you could only add new methods to existing types using static classes and this keyword in the first parameter. Now, with the new extension member syntax, you can also define extension properties, indexers, and even static extension members, making it possible to extend types in much more natural and expressive ways.

What Are Extension Members?

Extension members let you add new capabilities to existing types without modifying their source code or creating derived types. This is especially useful when working with interfaces or third-party libraries. The new syntax allows you to group related extension members together and write code that feels like it's part of the type itself.

Syntax Overview

The new syntax uses an extension block inside a static class. Within this block, you can declare:

- **Extension properties:** Add new properties to a type.

- **Extension indexers:** Add indexer access to types that don't have it.

- **Extension methods:** Continue to add methods as before, but with a cleaner grouping.

- **Static extension members:** Add static-like methods or properties that can be called directly on the type.

This approach makes your code more organized and expressive, especially when building utility libraries or domain-specific APIs.

Extension Property for Data Validation

Suppose you often work with string values that represent email addresses. You can add an extension property to quickly check if a string looks like a valid email:

```
public static class StringExtensions
{
    extension(string value)
    {
        public bool IsEmail =>
            !string.IsNullOrEmpty(value) &&
            value.Contains('@') &&
            value.IndexOf('.') > value.IndexOf('@');
    }
}

// Usage:
string email = "user@example.com";
Console.WriteLine(email.IsEmail); // True
```

This property can be used on any string to check its format in a readable way.

Extension Indexer for Dictionary Default Values

Imagine you want to safely get values from a dictionary, returning a default if the key is missing. You can add an extension indexer:

```
public static class DictionaryExtensions
{
    extension<TKey, TValue>(IDictionary<TKey, TValue> dict)
    {
        public TValue this[TKey key, TValue defaultValue] =>
            dict.TryGetValue(key, out var value) ? value : defaultValue;
    }
}

// Usage:
var settings = new Dictionary<string, string> { ["theme"] = "dark" };
Console.WriteLine(settings["theme", "light"]); // dark
Console.WriteLine(settings["font", "Arial"]); // Arial
```

This makes dictionary access safer and more concise.

Why Is This Important?

With extension members, you can now:

- Write more natural, readable code by using properties and indexers as if they were native to the type.

- Group all extensions for a type in a single place, reducing repetition and improving maintainability.

- Add static utilities directly to types, making APIs more discoverable and intuitive for consumers.

The *field* Keyword for Auto-Properties

C# 14 introduces a small but incredibly helpful feature: the `field` keyword, which gives you direct access to the compiler-generated backing field of an auto-implemented property right inside your property accessors. This means you can now add custom logic to your property's `get` or `set` without needing to declare a separate private variable, making your code cleaner and easier to maintain.

Why Is This Useful?

Before C# 14, if you wanted to add validation or extra logic to a property, you had to declare a private field and then write both the property and the field, which could get repetitive and cluttered. For example, if you wanted to make sure a `string` property was never set to null, you'd have to do something like this:

```
private string _message;
public string Message
{
    get => _message;
    set => _message = value ?? throw new ArgumentNullException(nameo
    f(value));
}
```

With the new `field` keyword, you can simplify this code and let the compiler handle the backing storage:

```
public string Message
{
    get;
    set => field = value ?? throw new ArgumentNullException(nameof(value));
}
```

Now, you get the benefits of auto-properties and still have room for validation or other logic, all without extra boilerplate code.

How Does It Work?

The `field` keyword in C# 14 is a contextual keyword designed to make property logic cleaner and more concise by giving you direct access to the compiler-generated backing field of an auto-implemented property, but only inside the property's accessors (the `get`, `set`, or `init` blocks).

When you declare a property using the standard auto-property syntax, such as `public string Name { get; set; }`, the compiler automatically creates a hidden variable (the backing field) to store the value. You never see or interact with this field directly—unless you switch to the new `field` keyword. With C# 14, you can now write custom logic in your property's accessors and refer to the backing field simply as field. For example, in the setter, you might validate or transform the incoming value before assigning it to the backing field, all without declaring your own private variable.

The `field` keyword only works inside the accessor of the property it belongs to, ensuring there's no confusion elsewhere in your class. If you use `field` in the `get` accessor, you're reading the current value stored by the property; if you use it in the `set` accessor, you're assigning a new value to that same hidden storage. This approach allows you to mix and match: you can use auto-accessors (`get;` or `set;`) for one part of the property and a custom accessor with field for the other, or you can use `field` in both.

If you ever have a variable named field in your class, C# will distinguish between your variable and the contextual keyword. You can use `@field` or `this.field` to refer to your own variable, while `field` on its own will always mean the auto-property's backing field inside the accessor.

In summary, the `field` keyword lets you keep the simplicity of auto-properties while adding custom logic exactly where you need it, all without extra boilerplate code or manual field declarations.

Practical Scenarios

You might want to trim whitespace from user input, enforce value ranges, or prevent unwanted assignments, all without writing extra fields. Here's another example, where you can make sure a property value is always positive:

```
public int Age
{
    get => field;
    set => field = value > 0 ? value : throw new ArgumentOutOfRangeException
(nameof(value), "Age must be positive.");
}
```

This keeps your code tidy and focused, with the logic right where it belongs.

Things to Watch Out For

If you already have a variable named `field` in your class, there could be confusion. In that case, you can use `@field` to refer to your own variable, or just rename it to avoid any mix-up. The `field` keyword only works inside property accessors, so you can't use it elsewhere in your class.

Null-Conditional Assignment

C# 14 introduces an elegant enhancement to how you handle null checks during assignments: you can now use the null-conditional operators `?.` and `?[]` on the left side of assignment statements. This means you can assign values to properties or elements only if the target object or collection is not null, all in a single, concise line of code.

Previously, if you wanted to assign a value to a property or an element but needed to ensure the object wasn't null, you had to write an explicit null check. For instance, you might have written:

```
if (customer is not null)
    customer.Order = GetCurrentOrder();
```

This approach works, but it adds extra lines and can clutter your code, especially when you have to perform similar checks in many places. With C# 14's null-conditional assignment, you can streamline this logic into a single line:

```
customer?.Order = GetCurrentOrder();
```

Here, the assignment to `Order` only occurs if customer is not null. If customer is null, the right side expression, `GetCurrentOrder()`, is never evaluated, so you avoid unnecessary work and potential side effects.

This feature also works with indexers. Suppose you have a dictionary that might be null, and you want to update a value only if the dictionary exists. Instead of checking for null explicitly, you can write:

```
scores?["math"] = 95;
```

Again, the assignment is performed only if scores is not null; otherwise, nothing happens and your program continues safely.

Null-conditional assignment isn't limited to simple assignment (=). It also supports compound assignments like +=, -=, and *=, so you can update values in place, as long as the target object or collection is not null. For example:

```
customer?.Total += 10;
```

This line will add 10 to the `Total` property only if customer is not null. However, increment and decrement operators (++ and --) are not supported in this context.

One of the key benefits of null-conditional assignment is that it makes your code cleaner and reduces the risk of null reference exceptions. You can chain these assignments through deeply nested objects as well. For example, if you have a chain of objects and want to set a value only if all are not null, you can write:

```
m?.A?.B?.C?.D = "Foo Bar";
```

This assignment will happen only if each object in the chain is not null, eliminating the need for multiple nested null checks.

In summary, null-conditional assignment in C# 14 brings a modern, concise way to handle optional assignments, making your code both safer and easier to read. It is especially useful in scenarios involving optional objects, deeply nested structures, or collections that may or may not be present at runtime.

nameof with Unbound Generic Types

C# 14 introduces a subtle but powerful enhancement to the `nameof` operator: you can now use it with unbound generic types, such as `List<>` or `Dictionary<,>`, to obtain the name of the generic type definition as a string without specifying any type arguments. This makes code that relies on type names—like logging, diagnostics, code generation, or source generators—cleaner and easier to maintain.

What Are Unbound Generic Types?

An unbound generic type refers to the generic type definition itself, without any concrete type arguments. For example, `List<>` is an unbound generic type, while `List<int>` is a closed generic type. Similarly, `Dictionary<,>` represents the generic definition for a dictionary with two type parameters.

How Does *nameof* Work with Unbound Generics?

Before C# 14, you could only use `nameof` with closed generic types, such as `nameof(List<int>)`, which would return `List`. However, trying `nameof(List<>)` would result in a compile-time error. With C# 14, you can now write:

```
Console.WriteLine(nameof(List<>));        // Output: List
Console.WriteLine(nameof(Dictionary<,>)); // Output: Dictionary
```

This feature also works with generic type members. For example, if you have a generic class with a property, you can write this:

```
class MyGeneric<T>
{
    public int Count { get; }
}

Console.WriteLine(nameof(MyGeneric<>.Count)); // Output: Count
```

This evaluates to the member's name, just as it would with a closed generic type.

Why Is This Useful?

Using `nameof` with unbound generic types helps you avoid hardcoding type names in your code, making it more refactor-safe and less error-prone. This is especially valuable when writing libraries, frameworks, or tools that work with generic types but do not require the specific type arguments. For example, you might want to log the name of a generic type in an error message or use it for metadata in source generators, all without needing to specify a concrete type.

Limitations

This new capability is limited to fully unbound generic types. You cannot use `nameof` with partially unbound types, such as `Dictionary<int,>`, nor can you nest unbound types as type arguments to other generics, like `A<B<>>`. These scenarios are not supported and have little practical benefit over using the generic definition directly.

The ability to use `nameof` with unbound generic types in C# 14 makes your code cleaner, safer, and more maintainable, especially when working with generic type definitions in reflection, diagnostics, or tooling scenarios. This small but meaningful improvement helps you write code that is easier to refactor and less prone to errors.

Lambda Parameter Modifiers

C# 14 brings a significant boost to how you write lambda expressions by allowing you to use parameter modifiers such as `ref`, `in`, `out`, `scoped`, and `ref readonly` directly in lambda parameters, even when you don't specify the parameter types explicitly. This change makes lambda syntax more concise and expressive, especially when you want to work with references, outputs, or scoped values.

What Changed in C# 14?

In earlier versions of C#, if you wanted to use a modifier like `ref` or `out` in a lambda, you had to write out the full type of each parameter. This often led to repetitive and verbose code, especially when the types could be inferred from the delegate or expression tree you were assigning the lambda to. With C# 14, you can now declare these modifiers right in the parameter list, and the compiler will figure out the types for you based on the context.

How Does It Work?

Now, you can write a lambda with a modifier directly in the parameter list, such as `(ref value) => { ... }` or `(out result) => { ... }`, and the compiler will infer the type from the delegate or method signature you're targeting. This works for all the supported modifiers:

- **ref:** Passes the argument by reference, allowing the lambda to modify the caller's variable.

- **out:** Passes the argument as an output, requiring the lambda to assign a value before returning.

- **in:** Passes the argument by reference as read-only, letting the lambda read but not modify the value.

- **ref readonly:** Passes the argument by reference in a read-only way, useful for certain value types.

- **scoped:** Indicates the parameter is scoped to the caller, preventing it from being captured or stored beyond the lambda's execution.

Practical Benefits

This new flexibility means you can write cleaner, less repetitive code, especially when working with APIs or delegates that use these modifiers. For example, when processing data in place, managing output parameters, or working with stack-only types, your lambdas become more readable and maintainable. The compiler's type inference handles the details, so you can focus on the logic rather than boilerplate.

Limitations

It's important to note that the `params` modifier is not supported in this new syntax. If you need a lambda with a `params` parameter, you must still specify the parameter's type explicitly. This ensures clarity when dealing with variable-length argument lists.

Practical Examples

C# 14 lets lambda expressions use `ref`, `out`, `in`, `scoped`, and `ref readonly` directly in parameter lists without explicit types, which keeps code concise while preserving full control over parameter passing and lifetimes. This section outlines some practical, real-world examples that demonstrate each modifier in action using the new concise syntax, with types inferred from the target delegate or method signature.

Ref: **In-place updates to caller data**

Scenario: Adjust an order total in-place during a discount pass.

```
delegate void ApplyDiscount(ref decimal total);

ApplyDiscount discount = (ref total) =>
{
    if (total > 100m) total -= 10m;
};

decimal due = 125m;
discount(ref due);
```

This uses `ref` to mutate the caller's variable in-place through the lambda, relying on the delegate signature for type inference.

Out: **try-parse flow without repeating types**

Scenario: Parse a configuration value once and flow the parsed result to the caller.

```
delegate bool TryParse<T>(string text, out T value);

TryParse<int> parsePort = (text, out value) => int.TryParse(text,
out value);

if (parsePort("8080", out var port))
{
    // use port
}
```

The lambda omits explicit parameter types while still using out, which the compiler infers from the delegate.

In: Read-only reference for large structs

Scenario: Log metrics from a large struct snapshot without copying.

```
public readonly struct Metrics
{
    public readonly double Cpu;
    public readonly double Mem;
    public Metrics(double cpu, double mem) { Cpu = cpu; Mem = mem; }
}

delegate void LogMetrics(in Metrics m);

LogMetrics log = (in m) =>
{
    Console.WriteLine($"CPU={m.Cpu:F1} MEM={m.Mem:F1}");
};
```

The in modifier passes a readonly reference to avoid copying large value types while preventing accidental mutation in the lambda.

ref readonly: Reference semantics without mutation

Scenario: Use a ref readonly parameter to expose reference identity while guaranteeing immutability.

```
delegate double Score(ref readonly ReadOnlySpan<double> window);

Score avg = (ref readonly window) =>
```

```
{
    double sum = 0;
    foreach (var x in window) sum += x;
    return window.Length == 0 ? 0 : sum / window.Length;
};
```

This combines reference semantics with read-only safety; the compiler enforces non-mutation of the referenced data.

***Scoped*: Enforce lifetime rules for stack-only data**

Scenario: Process a Span<int> that must not escape the lambda (no capturing or storing).

```
delegate int Sum(scoped Span<int> data);

Sum sum = (scoped data) =>
{
    var total = 0;
    foreach (var n in data) total += n;
    return total;
};
```

The scoped modifier ensures that data (a stack-only Span<int>) can't be captured beyond the call, aligning with safe lifetime rules for ref struct types.

First-Class *Span<T>* and *ReadOnlySpan<T>* Support

C# 14 introduces first-class support for Span<T> and ReadOnlySpan<T>, making high-performance memory access easier and safer than ever before. These types allow you to work with slices of memory—such as arrays, strings, or buffers—without unnecessary allocations, and now the language offers new implicit conversions that streamline their use in everyday code.

What Are *Span<T>* and *ReadOnlySpan<T>*?

Span<T> is a stack-only, ref struct that represents a contiguous region of memory. It allows you to safely and efficiently manipulate data without copying or allocating new memory. ReadOnlySpan<T> is its immutable counterpart, letting you read from memory regions without the risk of modification.

New Implicit Conversions in C# 14

C# 14 expands the set of implicit conversions involving spans, making it much simpler to pass arrays, strings, and even other spans to APIs expecting Span<T> or ReadOnlySpan<T>. The compiler now recognizes the following conversions:

- **Array to Span:** Any one-dimensional array (T[ ]) can be implicitly converted to Span<T>.

- **Array to ReadOnlySpan:** Arrays can also implicitly convert to ReadOnlySpan<T>.

- **Span to ReadOnlySpan:** A mutable Span<T> can be used wherever a ReadOnlySpan<T> is expected.

- **String to ReadOnlySpan<char>:** Strings can be implicitly treated as read-only spans of characters, making string slicing and processing more efficient.

These conversions eliminate the need for explicit casts or helper methods, making your code cleaner and more efficient.

Efficient Buffer Manipulation

Suppose you want to zero out a segment of an integer array. With implicit span conversions, you can write the following:

```
void ZeroOut(Span<int> buffer, int start, int length)
{
    buffer.Slice(start, length).Clear();
}

int[] data = { 1, 2, 3, 4, 5, 6, 7, 8 };
ZeroOut(data, 2, 3); // data now contains {1, 2, 0, 0, 0, 6, 7, 8}
```

Here, the int[ ] array is automatically converted to a Span<int>, and the Clear method efficiently zeroes the specified segment without any extra allocations.

String Processing Without Allocations

You can now pass a string directly to a method expecting a ReadOnlySpan<char>, enabling fast, allocation-free substring operations:

```
void PrintFirstWord(ReadOnlySpan<char> text)
{
    int space = text.IndexOf(' ');
```

```
    var word = space == -1 ? text : text.Slice(0, space);
    Console.WriteLine(word.ToString());
}
```

```
string sentence = "Hello world from C# 14";
PrintFirstWord(sentence); // Output: Hello
```

No need for .AsSpan() or explicit casting—the string is seamlessly treated as a span.

Custom Extension Methods on Spans

With implicit conversions, you can write extension methods for ReadOnlySpan<T> and call them directly on arrays, spans, or strings:

```
public static class SpanExtensions
{
    public static bool EndsWithZero(this ReadOnlySpan<int> span)
        => span.Length > 0 && span[^1] == 0;
}
```

```
int[] numbers = { 1, 2, 3, 0 };
Console.WriteLine(numbers.EndsWithZero()); // Output: True
```

The array is automatically converted, so your extension method works everywhere.

Why Does This Matter?

These new conversions make high-performance, allocation-free programming in C# much more accessible. You can process data, slice buffers, and write efficient algorithms without worrying about manual conversions or extra overloads. This is especially valuable in scenarios like parsing, binary encoding, image processing, and network programming, where every allocation counts.

Partial Events and Constructors

C# 14 introduces a powerful new way to organize and structure your code: the ability to declare instance constructors and events as partial members within partial classes. This feature is particularly helpful in large projects, code generation scenarios, or when working in teams, as it allows you to split the definition and implementation of constructors and events across multiple files for better clarity and maintainability.

What Are Partial Constructors?

Partial constructors let you split a class constructor into two separate declarations within a partial class. One part, known as the *defining declaration,* provides just the constructor's signature and ends with a semicolon, while the other part, called the *implementing declaration,* contains the actual code for the constructor. Both declarations must match exactly in terms of parameter types and names, and they must be placed in the same partial class.

For example, in a codebase where some files are auto-generated and others are maintained by developers, the auto-generated part might declare the constructor, while the developer's file provides the implementation. This separation makes it easier to extend generated code without modifying it directly, which is especially useful for frameworks, UI designers, or source generators.

Only the implementing declaration can include constructor initializers such as : `base()` or : `this()`, and if you use the primary constructor syntax (where parameters are declared in the class header), it can only appear in one partial declaration.

What Are Partial Events?

Partial events allow you to split the declaration and implementation of events in a partial class. The defining declaration is a simple, field-like event declaration, while the implementing declaration provides the add and remove accessors that control what happens when handlers are attached or detached. This is especially useful for separating event logic—such as instrumentation, logging, or platform-specific event handling— from the main event declaration.

Just like with partial constructors, both parts must match in event type and name, and there must be exactly one defining and one implementing declaration in the same partial class. The defining declaration acts as a placeholder, while the implementing declaration contains the logic for managing event subscriptions.

Why Does This Matter?

The ability to declare constructors and events as partial members brings several benefits:

- **Separation of concerns:** You can keep auto-generated code and custom logic in separate files, making your codebase easier to maintain and extend.

- **Better tooling support:** Source generators and frameworks can define what needs to exist, while developers provide the custom implementation.

- **Cleaner organization:** Large classes can be split logically across files, helping teams work independently without merge conflicts.

This enhancement rounds out the partial class feature set in C#, making it possible to split nearly any member type across files for maximum flexibility and clarity.

Partial Constructor for Plugin Initialization

Suppose you're building a plugin system where a code generator creates the basic plugin structure, but you want to add custom initialization logic yourself.

```
public partial class Plugin
{
    // Defining declaration: just the signature
    public partial Plugin(string pluginName, string version);
}

public partial class Plugin
{
    // Implementing declaration: provides the logic
    public partial Plugin(string pluginName, string version)
    {
        if (string.IsNullOrWhiteSpace(pluginName))
            throw new ArgumentException("Plugin name cannot be empty.",
            nameof(pluginName));
        Version = version ?? "1.0.0";
        Console.WriteLine($"Plugin '{pluginName}' initialized with version
        {Version}.");
    }

    public string Version { get; }
}
```

This setup allows the generated file to declare what constructors must exist, while the developer file provides the actual behavior.

Partial Event for Custom Notification Handling

Suppose you want to allow a source generator to declare an event, but you want to customize how subscribers are managed.

```csharp
public partial class Notifier
{
    // Defining declaration: just the event signature
    public partial event EventHandler? Alert;
}

public partial class Notifier
{
    private List<EventHandler> _subscribers = new();

    // Implementing declaration: custom add/remove logic
    public partial event EventHandler? Alert
    {
        add
        {
            if (value != null && !_subscribers.Contains(value))
                _subscribers.Add(value);
        }
        remove
        {
            if (value != null)
                _subscribers.Remove(value);
        }
    }

    public void RaiseAlert()
    {
        foreach (var handler in _subscribers)
            handler?.Invoke(this, EventArgs.Empty);
    }
}
```

This gives you full control over how event handlers are stored and invoked, which can be useful for custom notification or filtering scenarios.

Recap of the Most Impactful C# 14 Changes

C# 14 delivers a set of enhancements that make the language more expressive, concise, and developer-friendly, building on its tradition of continuous improvement. This section recaps the most impactful changes introduced in this version.

Extension Members

C# 14 takes extension methods to a new level by allowing you to define extension properties, indexers, and static extension members within extension blocks. This means you can now add reusable logic—such as properties and indexers—directly to existing types, making your code more organized and expressive without modifying the original type or creating derived classes.

Null-Conditional Assignment

Assignments can now use the null-conditional operators ?. and ?[] on the left side, letting you assign values only if the target is not null. This makes your code cleaner and safer, reducing the need for repetitive null checks and minimizing the risk of null reference exceptions.

nameof with Unbound Generic Types

The `nameof` operator now supports unbound generic types, such as `List<>` and `Dictionary<,>`. This allows you to reference generic type names in a safer, more maintainable way, which is especially useful for logging, diagnostics, and code generation tasks.

First-Class *Span<T>* and *ReadOnlySpan<T>* Support

Implicit conversions between arrays, spans, and strings make high-performance, allocation-free programming easier and more accessible. This update is particularly valuable for scenarios involving data processing, parsing, or buffer management, where efficiency and safety are crucial.

Lambda Parameter Modifiers

You can now use parameter modifiers like `ref`, `in`, `out`, `scoped`, and `ref readonly` directly in lambda expressions without specifying explicit types. This change streamlines functional programming patterns and makes code involving reference or output parameters much more readable and concise.

The *field* Keyword for Auto-Properties

The new `field` keyword allows you to access the compiler-generated backing field of an auto-property directly inside property accessors. This simplifies property logic, enabling validation or transformation without declaring separate private fields, and it keeps your code tidy and focused.

Partial Constructors and Events

C# 14 expands partial type support by allowing constructors and events to be declared as partial members. This makes it easier to organize large codebases, separate generated and custom logic, and collaborate on complex projects without merge conflicts or code duplication.

File-Based Apps and Scripting

With the new `dotnet run` support for standalone `.cs` files, C# becomes more approachable for scripting, prototyping, and automation. File-level directives like `#:package`, `#:sdk`, and `#:property` allow you to manage dependencies and configuration directly in your script, making C# a practical choice for quick utilities and learning scenarios.

C# 14's enhancements focus on making everyday development more productive, safe, and enjoyable. By embracing these new features, you can write cleaner, more efficient code and take full advantage of the modern .NET ecosystem.

CHAPTER 4

Modern APIs with ASP.NET Core 10

Introduction

APIs have always been at the heart of ASP.NET. From the early days of ASP.NET SOAP web services, through the unified ASP.NET Core era, and now with the rise of minimal APIs, the framework has continually adapted to new developer needs and industry trends. In the last few major .NET releases, we've seen a remarkable acceleration in how API development is approached, both in terms of performance and developer experience.

ASP.NET Web API is one of the most loved backend frameworks (based on a StackOverflow annual survey). The power and flexibility of minimal APIs and controller-based APIs mean you can easily create any type of software you can imagine.

.NET 10 marks a particularly interesting point in this journey. The ASP.NET team is not just iterating, but reimagining how APIs can be built, tested, and documented. Minimal APIs, introduced in .NET 6, have matured rapidly and are now a first-class citizen, offering a streamlined, function-first approach to building HTTP endpoints. At the same time, controller-based APIs remain fully supported and continue to receive meaningful improvements, making this a pivotal moment for teams deciding how to structure new projects or modernize existing ones.

Let's set the stage for this chapter by exploring the two primary approaches for building APIs in ASP.NET Core: Minimal APIs and Controller-based APIs.

© Kajetan Duszyński 2025
K. Duszyński, *.NET 10 Revealed*, https://doi.org/10.1007/979-8-8688-1889-9_4

Minimal APIs vs. Controller-based APIs: When and Why

Minimal APIs are all about simplicity and speed. They allow you to define HTTP endpoints with just a few lines of code. This approach is ideal for:

- Microservices and lightweight HTTP services

- Prototyping or proof-of-concept projects

- Applications where you want minimal ceremony and maximum performance

Scenarios where dependency injection and advanced routing are still needed, but without the full MVC stack

Minimal APIs shine when you want to get up and running quickly, reduce boilerplate code, and keep your codebase lean.

Controller-based APIs, on the other hand, follow the traditional MVC/Web API pattern. They provide:

- Clear separation of concerns via controllers, actions, and models

- Rich support for features like filters, model binding, validation, and conventions

- Easier migration paths for existing ASP.NET Core or legacy Web API projects

- More structure for large teams or complex applications

Controller-based APIs are still the best choice when you need to maintain existing MVC features. They're also preferred in codebases where convention-based organization are priorities.

Where Does .NET 10 Fit In?

The most exciting part of the current evolution is that you don't have to choose one or the other. .NET 10 makes it easier than ever to mix and match minimal APIs and controllers in the same application. You can start simple and scale up to a more structured approach as your needs grow, or you can modernize legacy controllers while adopting minimal APIs for new features.

The rest of this chapter dives deep into the latest API-wide improvements, explores what's new for both minimal APIs and controllers, and shows you how to leverage .NET 10's features to build robust, modern APIs-no matter which approach you prefer.

About the Sample Application

To make this chapter practical and relatable, it uses a sample application that's both familiar and flexible: a *task management system*. This isn't just a "hello world" API—it's a real-world, multi-user to-do list and task tracker, designed to demonstrate the latest features in .NET 10 without overwhelming you with unnecessary business logic.

Why Use a Task Management System?

Task management is a classic scenario for APIs: it involves users, tasks, assignments, comments, and attachments and covers most of the CRUD (Create, Read, Update, and Delete) patterns and relationships you'll encounter in modern web development. It's also easy to extend with features like filtering, sorting, authentication, and notifications, making it ideal for illustrating new .NET and ASP.NET Core capabilities.

Application Structure

This sample app is intentionally straightforward, so you can focus on .NET 10 features rather than wrestling with convoluted architecture. Here's how it's structured:

- **Users:** People who can create, assign, and complete tasks.
- **Tasks:** The core entity, with fields like title, description, due date, status, and priority.
- **Comments:** Linked to tasks, allowing collaboration and discussion.
- **Attachments:** Optional files or images associated with tasks.
- **(Optional) groups or projects**: For organizing tasks if you want to demonstrate more advanced relationships.

The API exposes endpoints for all the standard operations: creating and updating tasks, assigning users, adding comments, and managing attachments. You'll see minimal APIs and controller-based APIs, which illustrate how each approach handles these operations and how you can mix and match them in a modern .NET 10 codebase.

Design Principles

The guiding principle behind this sample application is clarity over complexity. Every code example is crafted to be straightforward and easy to follow, so you can focus on the innovations introduced in .NET 10 rather than getting dragged into some crazy business logic or unnecessary abstractions. Readability and adaptability are prioritized, making it simple for you to take these patterns and apply them to your own projects.

While the application architecture uses familiar layers—such as Data Transfer Objects (DTOs), services, and repositories—these are introduced only when they help illustrate a new feature or best practice. There's no over-engineering here; each layer exists to serve a purpose, not to add ceremony. This approach ensures that you see real-world, maintainable patterns without the distraction of excessive boilerplate code.

As you progress through the chapter, you'll see how the application can be naturally extended with authentication, OpenAPI documentation, or robust integration testing. Each enhancement is introduced in context, so you not only learn about the new capabilities in .NET 10, but also see how they fit into a practical, production-ready API. This balance allows you to build confidence in both the framework and your own codebase as you explore the latest ASP.NET Core features.

Using the Sample App

The task management system evolves step by step throughout this chapter:

- Starting with a minimal API for basic task CRUD.

- Adding controller-based endpoints for more complex scenarios.

- Layering in authentication, OpenAPI, and integration testing.

- Refactoring code to showcase new .NET 10 features.

By the end, you'll have a working, modern API that's easy to extend and ready for production patterns, or to use as a template in your own projects.

API-Wide Improvements in .NET 10

Integration Testing Enhancements

Integration testing is a critical part of any robust API development workflow, and .NET 10 brings a significant quality-of-life improvement for teams using top-level statements. This is a pattern now common in both minimal APIs and modern controller-based projects.

In earlier versions of .NET, top-level statements (where your application's entry point is written directly in `Program.cs` without an explicit `Program` class) made integration testing more challenging. The compiler-generated `Program` class and its `Main` method were not directly accessible by name, which complicated the use of `WebApplication Factory<TEntryPoint>` in integration test projects, especially when developers wanted to bootstrap their apps for end-to-end HTTP testing.

What's New in .NET 10?

Starting with .NET 10, the ASP.NET Core infrastructure now fully supports integration testing for applications using top-level statements. The generated `Program` class for top-level statements is now public by default in ASP.NET Core projects targeting .NET 10. This means you can reference `Program` directly as the entry point for your test host, just as you can with a traditional `Program` class. As a result, `WebApplicationFactory` `<Program>` works seamlessly for both minimal APIs and controller-based APIs, regardless of whether you use top-level statements or the classic `Main` method pattern.

Why It Matters

- **Consistency**: You no longer need to restructure your application or introduce extra boilerplate code just for testing. Minimal APIs and controllers can be tested using the same patterns.

- **Simplicity**: Integration tests can be written just as before, using `Web ApplicationFactory<Program>` and your preferred test framework (xUnit, NUnit, etc.), without worrying about the underlying entry point structure.

- **Modernization**: Teams can confidently adopt top-level statements for cleaner, more modern code, knowing that their testing strategy won't be disrupted.

Before .NET 10: The Workaround

Suppose you had a minimal API using top-level statements in `Program.cs`:

```
var builder = WebApplication.CreateBuilder(args);
var app = builder.Build();

app.MapGet("/tasks", () => new[] { "Task 1", "Task 2" });

app.Run();
```

In .NET 6/7/8/9, you couldn't reference a `Program` class directly in your test project, so you had to add boilerplate code like this:

```
// In Program.cs
public partial class Program { }

// In your test project:
public class TaskApiTests : IClassFixture<WebApplicationFactory
<Program>>
{
    // ...
}
```

This partial class, `Program` was a workaround to give your test project something to reference, but it was unintuitive and easy to forget, especially for new projects or teams refactoring to top-level statements.

After .NET 10: Seamless Integration

With .NET 10, the ASP.NET Core infrastructure now makes the compiler-generated `Program` class public by default for projects using top-level statements. This means you can reference `Program` directly in your test code, just as you would with a traditional `Main` method.

Here's the same minimal API, unchanged:

```
var builder = WebApplication.CreateBuilder(args);
var app = builder.Build();

app.MapGet("/tasks", () => new[] { "Task 1", "Task 2" });

app.Run();
```

And now your integration test can simply reference the generated `Program` class:

```
public class TaskApiTests : IClassFixture<WebApplicationFactory<Program>>
{
    private readonly WebApplicationFactory<Program> _factory;

    public TaskApiTests(WebApplicationFactory<Program> factory)
    {
        _factory = factory;
    }

    [Fact]
    public async Task GetTasks_ReturnsTasks()
    {
        var client = _factory.CreateClient();
        var response = await client.GetAsync("/tasks");
        response.EnsureSuccessStatusCode();
        var content = await response.Content.ReadAsStringAsync();
        Assert.Contains("Task 1", content);
    }
}
```

No more workarounds or partial class declarations—just straightforward, idiomatic testing.

OpenAPI Updates

OpenAPI 3.1 Support

OpenAPI is the standard for describing and documenting RESTful APIs. In .NET 10, ASP.NET Core introduces first-class support for generating OpenAPI 3.1 documents for both minimal APIs and controller-based APIs. This upgrade is more than just a version bump—it brings your API documentation in line with the latest JSON Schema standards and unlocks new levels of interoperability and tooling support.

What's New and Why It Matters

- **Full JSON Schema 2020-12 support:** OpenAPI 3.1 aligns with the latest JSON Schema, making your API contracts more precise and compatible with a wider range of tools and languages.

- **Nullable types handling:** Nullable types in your models (like `DateTime? DueDate`) are now represented as `"type": ["string", "null"]` in the schema, instead of the older `nullable: true` approach. This makes your API contracts clearer for client code generators and documentation tools.

- **Schema changes for numbers:** Integer and long properties may now appear in the OpenAPI document with a `pattern` field instead of just `type: integer`, depending on your JSON serializer settings. This can affect how clients validate or generate code for your API.

- **YAML support:** You can now generate your OpenAPI docs in YAML as well as JSON, making it easier to integrate with tools or workflows that prefer YAML.

- **Version selection:** OpenAPI 3.1 is the new default, but you can target 3.0 if you need to maintain compatibility with older tools.

Example

Suppose your task management API exposes a model like this:

```
public class TaskDto
{
    public int Id { get; set; }
    public string Title { get; set; }
    public string? Description { get; set; }
    public DateTime? DueDate { get; set; }
    public int Priority { get; set; }
}
```

With OpenAPI 3.1 enabled (the default in .NET 10), your generated schema for `DueDate` and `Description` will now look like this:

```
"DueDate": {
  "type": ["string", "null"],
  "format": "date-time"
},
"Description": {
  "type": ["string", "null"]
}
```

This is more accurate and standards-compliant than the old `nullable: true` property.

How to Use It

By default, when you add OpenAPI support in .NET 10, your documentation uses the 3.1 specification. If you need to target OpenAPI 3.0 (for compatibility), specify it explicitly.

Customizing OpenAPI Output

If you want to provide an example for your `TaskDto` schema, you'll need to update your schema transformer code to match the new OpenAPI/JSON Schema style.

Before (.NET 9):

```
options.AddSchemaTransformer((schema, context, cancellationToken) =>
{
    if (context.JsonTypeInfo.Type == typeof(TaskDto))
    {
        schema.Example = new OpenApiObject
        {
            ["id"] = new OpenApiInteger(1),
            ["title"] = new OpenApiString("Write documentation"),
            ["description"] = new OpenApiString("Complete the API docs for
            the project"),
            ["dueDate"] = new OpenApiString(DateTime.Now.AddDays(2).
            ToString("o")),
            ["priority"] = new OpenApiInteger(2)
        };
    }
```

```
    return Task.CompletedTask;
});
```

After (.NET 10):

```
options.AddSchemaTransformer((schema, context, cancellationToken) =>
{
    if (context.JsonTypeInfo.Type == typeof(TaskDto))
    {
        schema.Example = new JsonObject
        {
            ["id"] = 1,
            ["title"] = "Write documentation",
            ["description"] = "Complete the API docs for the project",
            ["dueDate"] = DateTime.Now.AddDays(2).ToString("o"),
            ["priority"] = 2
        };
    }
    return Task.CompletedTask;
});
```

Why This Matters to Your API

- **Better client code generation:** Tools like NSwag and OpenAPI
  Generator will create more accurate C# or TypeScript clients for your
  task models.

- **Clearer documentation:** Nullable fields and data types are described
  in a way that matches modern JSON Schema, reducing confusion for
  consumers of your API.

- **Future-proofing:** You're ready for the next wave of OpenAPI tooling
  and integrations, with no need for workarounds or custom hacks.

Generating OpenAPI Documents in YAML Format

.NET 10 introduces a convenient new feature for API developers: the ability to serve your OpenAPI (Swagger) document in YAML format, in addition to the traditional JSON output. YAML is often preferred for its readability, especially in environments where configuration files and API contracts are reviewed or edited by hand. It's more concise, omits unnecessary braces and quotes, and supports multiline strings, making it ideal for longer descriptions or documentation.

Enabling YAML Output

Serving your OpenAPI document as YAML is as simple as specifying a `.yaml` or `.yml` suffix when mapping the OpenAPI endpoint in your application. For example, in your task management API, you can add the following line to your endpoint configuration:

```
app.MapOpenApi("/openapi/{documentName}.yaml");
```

With this in place, you (or your API consumers) can now access the OpenAPI specification in YAML format by navigating to an endpoint like so:

```
GET http://localhost:5000/openapi/v1.yaml
```

This is especially useful for teams that want to integrate with tools or processes that prefer YAML, or for those who want a more human-friendly format for reviewing and sharing API contracts.

Current Limitations

YAML output is currently only available when serving the OpenAPI document at runtime from the OpenAPI endpoint.

Build-time generation of YAML documents is planned for a future .NET release but is not yet available.

General API Improvements

One of the most welcome quality-of-life improvements for API developers in recent .NET versions is the introduction of route template syntax highlighting and tooling support in Visual Studio and VS Code. This feature is now available for both minimal APIs and controller-based APIs, making route definitions clearer, reducing errors, and speeding up development.

Previously, route templates—strings like `"/tasks/{id:int}"` and `"/users/{userId}/tasks"`—were just plain text in your editor. If you made a typo or misused a route parameter, you'd only find out at runtime or after a failed HTTP request. With .NET's enhanced route tooling, your IDE now provides the following:

- **Syntax highlighting** for route templates, making parameters, constraints, and tokens visually distinct.

- **Autocomplete** for route parameters and constraints, so you can quickly insert the right syntax.

- **Route analyzers and fixers** that alert you to common mistakes (like a catch-all parameter not being last, or an optional parameter with a default value).

- **Consistent support** across minimal APIs, controllers, Razor pages, and Blazor routing.

Why It Matters

For complex APIs—like the chapter's task management system, where you might have endpoints such as `/tasks/{id:int}/comments/{commentId}` or `/users/{userId}/tasks`—route templates can get tricky. Syntax highlighting and tooling help you:

- Instantly spot errors or inconsistencies in your routes.

- Understand immediately which parts of the route are parameters, constraints, or tokens.

- Refactor and rename route parameters with confidence, knowing your IDE will catch mismatches.

Example in Practice

Suppose you define a minimal API endpoint like this:

```
app.MapGet("/tasks/{id:int}/comments/{commentId}", (int id, int
commentId) =>
{
    // Fetch and return the comment for a specific task
});
```

Or, in a controller:

```
[HttpGet("/tasks/{id:int}/comments/{commentId}")]
public IActionResult GetComment(int id, int commentId)
{
    // Fetch and return the comment for a specific task
}
```

With route template syntax highlighting enabled, your editor will visually distinguish:

- `{id:int}` as a route parameter with an integer constraint

- `{commentId}` as another route parameter

- Static segments like `/tasks/` and `/comments/`

If you accidentally write `/tasks/{id:int}/comments/{commentId:int?}` and put an optional parameter before a required one, the analyzer will flag this as an error before you run your app.

How Does It Work?

This feature leverages the `StringSyntax` attribute (introduced in .NET 7 and improved in .NET 8/10) and, in JetBrains Rider, the `RouteTemplateAttribute`. The tooling recognizes route templates in your code, providing colorization, completion, and validation in real time.

Minimal APIs Deep Dive

Validation Support in Minimal APIs

One of the biggest pain points for developers using minimal APIs in previous .NET versions was the lack of built-in model validation—a feature that's long been standard in controller-based APIs. With .NET 10, this gap has finally been closed: Minimal APIs now support automatic request validation using familiar data annotations and validation interfaces, making it easier than ever to ensure that your API only accepts valid data.

Of course, for a long time this has been covered by adding third-party libraries like Fluent Validation. Now it is covered in .NET 10.

How Does It Work?

Validation in minimal APIs is now handled automatically for parameters bound from the query string, headers, or request body. You use the same `[Required]`, `[Range]`, `[EmailAddress]` attributes, as well as other attributes from the `System.ComponentModel.DataAnnotations` namespace that you're used to from MVC. For more complex scenarios, you can implement `IValidatableObject` or even create custom validation attributes.

When validation fails, the runtime returns a `400 Bad Request` response, including details about which fields failed and why. No extra code or manual checks required.

Enabling Validation

To enable validation in your minimal API project, simply register the validation services in your `Program.cs`:

```
builder.Services.AddValidation();
```

This single line configures the runtime to automatically discover and validate types used in your minimal API handlers.

Example: Validating Tasks in a Task Management API

Suppose you have a `TaskDto` for creating tasks, and you want to ensure that every task has a title and a due date in the future:

```
using System.ComponentModel.DataAnnotations;

public class TaskDto
{
    [Required]
    public string Title { get; set; }

    [FutureDate(ErrorMessage = "Due date must be in the future")]
    public DateOnly? DueDate { get; set; }
}
```

The FutureDate attribute is defined like so:

```
using System;
using System.ComponentModel.DataAnnotations;

public class FutureDateAttribute : ValidationAttribute
{
    public FutureDateAttribute(string errorMessage = "The date must be in
    the future.")
    {
        ErrorMessage = errorMessage;
    }

    protected override ValidationResult IsValid(object value,
    ValidationContext validationContext)
    {
        if (value == null)
            return ValidationResult.Success; // Let [Required] handle nulls
            if needed

        if (value is DateTime date)
        {
            if (date > DateTime.Now)
                return ValidationResult.Success;
            return new ValidationResult(ErrorMessage ?? $"The
            {validationContext.DisplayName} field must be a future date.");
        }
```

```
        return new ValidationResult("Invalid data type for
        FutureDateAttribute.");
    }
}
```

Now, you define your minimal API endpoint:

```
app.MapPost("/tasks", (TaskDto task) =>
{
    // If validation fails, a 400 Bad Request is returned automatically
    // If validation succeeds, the handler logic runs
    return Results.Ok(task);
});
```

If a client sends a request with a missing title or a past due date, the API will immediately respond with a detailed 400 error describing the validation issues.

Advanced: Disabling Validation for Specific Endpoints

If you need to opt out of automatic validation for a specific endpoint, you can do so with `.DisableValidation()`:

```
app.MapPost("/tasks/import", (TaskDto task) =>
{
    // Custom import logic, possibly skipping validation
    return Results.Ok(task);
})
.DisableValidation();
```

Custom Validation Logic

For even more control, implement `IValidatableObject` on your DTO or use custom attributes:

```
public class TaskDto : IValidatableObject
{
    [Required]
    public string Title { get; set; }
```

```csharp
public DateOnly? DueDate { get; set; }

public IEnumerable<ValidationResult> Validate(ValidationContext
validationContext)
{
    if (DueDate != null && DueDate < DateOnly.
    FromDateTime(DateTime.Today))
    {
        yield return new ValidationResult("Due date must be today or in
        the future", new[] { nameof(DueDate) });
    }
}
}
```

Why It Matters

- **Consistency:** You get the same validation experience in minimal APIs as in controllers, reducing surprises when switching between approaches.

- **Productivity:** No more writing manual validation logic or relying on third-party packages for common scenarios.

- **Clarity:** Clients receive clear, standardized error responses when they send invalid data.

Treating Empty Strings as Null for Nullable Value Types in Form Posts

A subtle but important improvement in .NET 10 minimal APIs is how form data binding treats empty strings when mapping to nullable value types. Historically, if a client submitted a form with an empty string for a field like DueDate, and your API expected a type such as DateTime?, the model binder would either fail to convert the empty string or might set it to a default value, leading to inconsistent or confusing results. This was a common pain point, especially for forms where users might intentionally leave fields blank to indicate "no value".

With .NET 10, minimal APIs now automatically convert empty strings to *null* for nullable value types when binding form data. This means if a user submits a form with an empty value for a nullable property, your endpoint will receive `null`—not an empty string or an invalid value. This behavior makes it much easier to distinguish between "no value provided" and "a value was provided," and it aligns minimal API behavior with what developers expect from MVC model binding.

Authentication and Authorization

What's New in .NET 10: Metrics

Why It Matters

In modern API-driven applications, authentication and authorization aren't just about security—they're also about observability and reliability. Real-world systems need to answer questions like these:

- Are users experiencing slow logins or frequent authentication failures?

- Are authorization policies being triggered as expected?

- How often are users being challenged or forbidden, and is this affecting user experience or indicating misconfiguration?

Without concrete metrics, diagnosing production issues or optimizing the authentication flow can feel like guesswork. For example, imagine a scenario in your task management system where users intermittently report being signed out or denied access to certain endpoints. Without metrics, you're left combing through logs or trying to reproduce the issue manually. With metrics, you can quickly spot spikes in `forbid` or `challenge` events, correlate them with recent deployments, and take targeted action.

Out-of-the-Box Auth Metrics in .NET 10

.NET 10 introduces a comprehensive set of built-in metrics for authentication and authorization events in ASP.NET Core. These metrics are automatically exposed and can be consumed by observability tools, dashboards, or command-line utilities like `dotnet-counters`. The new metrics include the following.

- Authentication metrics:

  - `aspnetcore.authentication.authenticate.duration`: A histogram of how long authentication takes per request.

  - `aspnetcore.authentication.challenges`: A count of authentication challenges issued (e.g., 401 responses).

  - `aspnetcore.authentication.forbids`: A count of forbidden responses (e.g., 403s when a user is authenticated but not authorized).

  - `aspnetcore.authentication.sign_ins` and `aspnetcore.authentication.sign_outs`: A count of sign-in and sign-out events per authentication scheme.

- Authorization metrics:

  - `aspnetcore.authorization.attempts`: A count of requests requiring authorization, with details about the policy, result, and user authentication state.

Each metric includes rich contextual attributes, such as the authentication scheme (bearer, cookies), the outcome (success, failure), and the error types if applicable.

Using Metrics for Monitoring and Diagnostics

These metrics are invaluable for real-time monitoring, diagnostics, and capacity planning. You can:

- **Detect bottlenecks:** If `authenticate.duration` spikes, you may have a slow external identity provider or a misconfigured token validator.

- **Spot misconfigurations:** A high rate of `forbids` or `challenges` could indicate missing policies or incorrect role assignments.

- **Audit sign-in/sign-out flows:** Unexpected surges in `sign_outs` might reveal issues with session management or user confusion.

- **Correlate with incidents:** Metrics can be visualized in dashboards (e.g., Azure Monitor, Prometheus/Grafana, Aspire) to correlate auth failures with deployments or traffic spikes.

Introducing and Measuring Auth Metrics

All these metrics are enabled by default in .NET 10 web applications. If your API uses standard authentication and authorization middleware, the metrics are already being emitted.

For quick, ad hoc investigations, use the dotnet-counters tool:

```
dotnet tool update -g dotnet-counters
dotnet-counters monitor -n YourApiProcess –counters
Microsoft.ASPNetCore.Authentication
```

For ongoing monitoring, integrate with a metrics backend (like Prometheus, Azure Monitor, or the Aspire dashboard).

Example: Adding and Visualizing Metrics in Your Task Management API

Suppose you're running a task management API with JWT Bearer authentication and role-based authorization for endpoints like GET /tasks/assign (admin only) and GET /tasks (authenticated users). You want to monitor:

- How long authentication takes (for login performance)
- How many requests are being challenged or forbidden (to spot misconfigurations)
- How often users are signing in and out

Step 1: Ensure standard ASP.NET Core authentication/authorization is configured.

No special code is needed for metrics—they're emitted automatically.

Step 2: Monitor with dotnet-counters or your dashboard.

```
dotnet-counters monitor -n TaskManagementApi --counters
Microsoft.AspNetCore.Authentication
```

Step 3: Investigate and interpret the metrics.

If you see a spike in aspnetcore.authentication.challenges, check if your frontend is sending expired tokens or if a new endpoint is missing [Authorize].

If `aspnetcore.authentication.authenticate.duration` increases, investigate external identity providers or recent code changes.

If `aspnetcore.authorization.attempts` shows many failures, review your policy configuration and user roles.

Step 4: Visualize in Aspire or another dashboard.

Set up widgets to track sign-in/out counts, challenge/forbid rates, and average authentication duration. Use these to alert on anomalies or trends.

When to Measure and Monitor

- **During development:** Spot configuration issues early.

- **In staging/preproduction:** Validate performance and policy coverage under load.

- **In production:** Detect regressions, security issues, or user experience problems in real time.

CHAPTER 5

Blazor in .NET 10: Modern Web UI, Productivity, and Experience

Introduction

Blazor is one of those technologies that seems to be a natural fit for the core of modern .NET. Following .NET's development from its early Windows-only days to its current cross-platform ecosystem will show you how every new wave introduces something that alters the way people develop software. Blazor is the epitome of this innovative spirit. Using C# and .NET instead of JavaScript to create interactive web apps is a huge advantage for both novice and seasoned developers.

Blazor stands out among other important .NET Frameworks because it helps anyone who is familiar with C# or has worked with .NET in the past understand web development. Using the same language, tools, and libraries on the client and server eliminates the need to switch between frameworks and languages. A smoother learning curve, fewer bugs, and less context switching result from this. Blazor is the most intuitive approach for many teams to create contemporary web applications, particularly those that have already made an investment in .NET.

Blazor is particularly interesting because of its adaptability. With Blazor WebAssembly, you can run your application entirely within the browser; with Blazor Server, you can just send UI updates to the browser while maintaining the logic on the server. Even better, Blazor Hybrid allows you to use the same codebase for both native desktop and mobile applications. One major benefit of this "one stack, many platforms" strategy is that it allows you to reach more users without having to modify your app for every device.

© Kajetan Duszyński 2025
K. Duszyński, *.NET 10 Revealed*, https://doi.org/10.1007/979-8-8688-1889-9_5

Blazor is a friendly starting point for novices. You can create a dynamic website without knowing JavaScript. There are numerous built-in features for forms, data binding, routing, and security, and the component-based model is simple to understand. Additionally, the tooling is robust. Project templates, scaffolding, and hot reload are features that Visual Studio and VS Code provide so you can see your changes as you build.

Developers with experience will recognize Blazor's role in .NET ecosystem. Your desktop, mobile, and web apps can all share code. You can connect to APIs, use well-known patterns for testing and deployment, and call preexisting .NET libraries. Blazor is designed with the dependability, efficiency, and security that businesses require for actual business applications.

The community of Blazor is expanding quickly. Every month, new components, resources, and best practices are made available, and with Microsoft's support, it is here to stay. Blazor gives you the power and flexibility of .NET in the browser, whether you are creating a straightforward website, an internal tool, or a sophisticated enterprise application.

Remember that Blazor is more than just a technical framework as you explore what is new in Blazor for .NET 10. Using your existing skills, you can create contemporary web apps more quickly, cleanly, and confidently than ever before.

Blazor in .NET 10: A Quick Overview

Blazor has emerged as a key component of the .NET ecosystem, enabling the development of dynamic, rich web applications with just C# and .NET. This section considers what Blazor is, how it came to be, and what .NET 10 is trying to accomplish for Blazor developers before diving into all the new features in the version.

Blazor is special because it allows you to run your web application in multiple ways. The most popular is Blazor WebAssembly, which uses WebAssembly technology to run your C# code directly in the browser. This implies that your application does not require a server connection for each user interaction and can function offline. Blazor Server, on the other hand, enables your app's logic to execute on the server, instantly updating the user interface in the browser. This method speeds up app loading and reduces download size, but it does necessitate a consistent server connection. Another option is Blazor Hybrid, which combines web and native code to provide the best of both worlds by allowing you to use the same Blazor components in native desktop and mobile apps.

Blazor's path has been quick and innovative. Blazor was initially an experiment to see if C# could actually run in a browser. Blazor grew up with the .NET platform as it transitioned from being Windows-only to being cross-platform. Better performance, simpler state management, and additional tools for creating practical applications were all brought about by each .NET release. Blazor was used by developers for everything from dashboards to fully functional business systems. Microsoft paid attention to user feedback and improved Blazor's functionality and power with each release.

Blazor is now receiving yet another significant boost with .NET 10. This release's primary objectives are to improve Blazor apps' speed, reliability, and ease of development and maintenance. The Blazor script is now served as a static web asset, meaning it is automatically compressed and fingerprinted, which is one of the headline changes. This significantly lowers the download size and improves caching, giving your users a quicker experience from the beginning. Additionally, .NET 10 enhances state management, component styling, navigation, and even real-time communication, making it simpler than ever to create responsive, modern web apps.

.NET 10 is exciting because it offers more than just new features. Whether you are developing your first app or managing a big, intricate system, the goal is to make Blazor a top option for web development. This release's enhancements are intended to help you work more efficiently, write less code, and provide your users with better experiences.

As you progress through this chapter, you will see how Blazor in .NET 10 expands on all of the previous developments while creating new possibilities for advancement. There has never been a better moment to discover what Blazor has to offer, regardless of your level of experience as a developer.

Performance and Resource Optimizations

Blazor Script as a static Web Asset

Web application performance has always been a major concern, and Blazor makes significant progress in this area with .NET 10. The way the Blazor script is now managed and provided to users is among the most significant modifications. Although this update may seem technical, it has a significant effect on how quickly and smoothly your apps load for users.

The primary JavaScript file that bootstraps your Blazor application, such as `blazor.web.js`, `blazor.server.js`, or `blazor.webassembly.js`, was used as an embedded resource from the ASP.NET Core shared framework in previous iterations of Blazor. This implied that it was not optimized with the same features as your other static files, such as fingerprinting or automatic compression. Because of this, users may download larger files than they need to and occasionally even outdated, cached versions of the script, which could result in unexpected behavior or bugs.

With .NET 10, this script is now served as a static web asset. This change brings two big benefits: compression and fingerprinting.

When a script file is compressed, it automatically reduces in size before being sent to the browser. The `blazor.web.js` file, for instance, has drastically decreased in size from 183 KB to just 43 KB. Your users will download a lot less data as a result, which is crucial for those using mobile devices or slower connections.

A unique hash is appended to the script's filename through fingerprinting, such as `blazor.webassembly.abcd1234.js`. This guarantees that the browser will always retrieve the most recent script when you release an updated version of your application, rather than inadvertently utilizing an outdated, cached version. A whole class of difficult-to-track bugs that can occur when browsers serve stale files are eliminated by this straightforward modification.

Impact on Load Times and Caching

What does all of this actually mean? Your Blazor apps will launch more quickly, particularly for users who are visiting for the first time or after you release an update. The script downloads faster because it is compressed and smaller. Additionally, browsers can aggressively cache the script because fingerprinting ensures that they always receive the correct version when something changes.

If you want to see the difference for yourself, you can measure load times before and after upgrading to .NET 10. Here's how to run a simple benchmark:

1. Build and publish your Blazor app with .NET 9 and note the size of the `blazor.web.js` or `blazor.webassembly.js` file in the published output.

2. Upgrade your app to .NET 10 and publish it again. Compare the new script file size.

3. Use your browser's developer tools (from the Network tab) to measure how long it takes to download the script in both versions.

4. Clear your browser cache between tests to get accurate results.

You should see a clear drop in both file size and download time after moving to .NET 10. If you want to go further, you can use tools like Lighthouse or WebPageTest to get more detailed performance metrics.

WebAssembly Runtime Diagnostics

A much more comprehensive set of runtime diagnostics is now available for Blazor WebAssembly apps in.NET 10, which makes it simpler to identify unexpected behavior, memory leaks, and performance problems directly in your browser. This section covers what can be done, how to set it up, and when to use these tools.

Setting Up WebAssembly Diagnostics

Before you can use tracing, memory dumps, or runtime metrics, you need to install the .NET WebAssembly build tools. Open your terminal and run this command:

```
dotnet workload install wasm-tools
```

This one-time setup gives your project everything it needs for advanced diagnostics.

Enabling Diagnostics in Your Project

You control diagnostics using MSBuild properties in your project file (`.csproj`). This section explains how to enable each feature.

Performance Tracing

Add these properties to your `.csproj` file to turn on tracing and instrumentation:

```
<PropertyGroup>
  <WasmPerfTracing>true</WasmPerfTracing>
  <WasmPerfInstrumentation>all</WasmPerfInstrumentation>
</PropertyGroup>
```

`<WasmPerfTracing>` enables support for WebAssembly performance tracing.

`<WasmPerfInstrumentation>` enables the sampling profiler and can be set to `all` for full instrumentation or to specific values for targeted tracing.

Runtime Metrics

To collect runtime metrics (like garbage collection, allocations, etc.), add the following:

```
<PropertyGroup>
  <MetricsSupport>true</MetricsSupport>
</PropertyGroup>
```

This enables the `System.Diagnostics.Metrics` API in your Blazor WebAssembly app.

EventPipe and EventSource Support

For full `EventPipe` support (which powers tracing and memory dumps), enable the following:

```
<PropertyGroup>
  <EventSourceSupport>true</EventSourceSupport>
</PropertyGroup>
```

This allows you to use `EventPipe`-based tools and APIs in your app.

Collecting Traces and Memory Dumps

Once you've enabled diagnostics, you can collect and analyze data. This section explains how.

CPU Tracing (Sampling Profiler)

From your browser's JavaScript console, you can trigger a CPU trace:

```
globalThis.getDotnetRuntime(0).collectCpuSamples({ durationSeconds: 60 });
```

This command collects CPU samples for 60 seconds. The output is a `.nettrace` file, which you can download and analyze using tools like PerfView or Visual Studio's Performance Profiler.

Memory Dumps (GC Heap Dump)

To capture a memory dump (heap snapshot), run this in the browser console:

```
globalThis.getDotnetRuntime(0).dumpHeap();
```

This will generate a heap dump file. Download it and open it with Visual Studio or the .NET GC Heap Dump tool to inspect object allocations, references, and potential memory leaks.

Runtime Metrics

With `<MetricsSupport>true</MetricsSupport>`, your app emits metrics that can be collected and visualized using compatible tools. You can instrument your code to emit custom metrics using the `System.Diagnostics.Metrics` API, or use built-in counters for things like garbage collection, thread pool usage, and more.

When and Why to Use These Tools

Tracing is best for finding out why your app is slow or which parts of your code are consuming the most CPU. Use it when you notice sluggish UI, long load times, or unexplained performance drops.

Memory dumps are essential if your app is using more memory over time, crashes with out-of-memory errors, or you suspect a memory leak. Dumps show you exactly what's in memory and what's holding onto it.

Runtime metrics let you monitor your app's health over time. Use them to spot trends, such as increasing memory usage, frequent garbage collections, or unusual allocation patterns.

Practical Workflow Example

1. Enable diagnostics in your `.csproj` as explained previously.

2. Build and run your Blazor WebAssembly app.

3. Open the browser's developer console and use the provided JavaScript commands to collect traces or memory dumps.

4. Download the resulting files and analyze them with PerfView, Visual Studio, or other .NET diagnostic tools.

5. Interpret the results to find slow methods, memory leaks, or inefficient code paths.

UI and Component Enhancements

With each new release, Blazor's user interface continues to improve, and .NET 10 offers some much-needed enhancements, especially for the QuickGrid component. One of the simplest ways to display tabular data in a web application is with QuickGrid in Blazor. You can now create richer, more interactive tables with less code and more control thanks to new features like dynamic row styling and more customizable column options.

QuickGrid Improvements in .NET 10

The New *RowClass* Parameter for Dynamic Row Styling

One of the standout features in this release is the new RowClass parameter. This allows you to set CSS classes on each row based on its data, making it simple to highlight, color, or otherwise style rows dynamically. Imagine you want to highlight overdue tasks in a to-do list or flag high-priority items in red. With RowClass, you can do this without writing a lot of custom code.

Here's a practical example:

```
@page "/"
@using Microsoft.AspNetCore.Components.QuickGrid

<h1>Your upcoming tasks</h1>
<QuickGrid Items="tasks" RowClass="GetRowClass">
    <PropertyColumn Property="@(t => t.Title)" Title="Task" />
    <PropertyColumn Property="@(t => t.DueDate)" Title="Due Date" />
    <PropertyColumn Property="@(t => t.Status)" Title="Status" />
</QuickGrid>
```

```
<style>
    .table-danger {
        background-color: #f8d7da;
    }
    .table-success {
        background-color: #d4edda;
    }
</style>

@code {
    private IQueryable<TaskItem> tasks = new[]
    {
        new TaskItem { Title = "Finish report", DueDate = DateTime.Today.
        AddDays(-1), Status = "Overdue" },
        new TaskItem { Title = "Email client", DueDate = DateTime.Today,
        Status = "Completed" },
        new TaskItem { Title = "Update docs", DueDate = DateTime.Today.
        AddDays(1), Status = "Pending" }
    }.AsQueryable();

    string GetRowClass(TaskItem task)
    {
        if (task.Status == "Overdue") return "table-danger";
        if (task.Status == "Completed") return "table-success";
        return "";
    }

    class TaskItem
    {
        public string Title { get; set; }
        public DateTime DueDate { get; set; }
        public string Status { get; set; }
    }
}
```

This approach lets you visually distinguish rows based on their status (see Figure 5-1), making your data grids much more user-friendly.

Your upcoming tasks

Task	Due Date	Status
Finish report	23.07.2025 00:00:00	Overdue
Email client	24.07.2025 00:00:00	Completed
Update docs	25.07.2025 00:00:00	Pending

Figure 5-1. *Marking rows based on their status*

Other Usability Tweaks: *CloseColumnOptionsAsync*

CloseColumnOptionsAsync is another useful addition. QuickGrid's column options
menu can be programmatically closed using this technique. Imagine that when a user
clicks Apply or Cancel in your user interface, a custom filter or settings panel should
close. By using this new technique, you can improve the user experience by making sure
the column options panel closes at the appropriate moment.

Here's how you might use this in a real app:

```
@page "/medals"
@rendermode InteractiveServer
@using Microsoft.AspNetCore.Components.QuickGrid

<div class="grid">
    <QuickGrid Items="@FilteredCountries" Pagination="@pagination"
    @ref="countriesGrid">
        <PropertyColumn Property="@((Country c) => c.Name)" Sortable="true"
        Class="country-name">
            <ColumnOptions>
                <div class="search-box">
                    <input type="search" autofocus @bind="nameFilter"
                            @bind:after="() => countriesGrid.
                            HideColumnOptionsAsync()"
                            placeholder="Country name..."/>
                </div>
            </ColumnOptions>
        </PropertyColumn>
```

```
        <PropertyColumn Property="@((Country c) => c.Medals.Gold)"
        Sortable="true" Align="Align.Right"/>
        <PropertyColumn Property="@((Country c) => c.Medals.Silver)"
        Sortable="true" Align="Align.Right"/>
        <PropertyColumn Property="@((Country c) => c.Medals.Bronze)"
        Sortable="true" Align="Align.Right"/>
        <PropertyColumn Property="@((Country c) => c.Medals.Total)"
        Sortable="true" Align="Align.Right">
        </PropertyColumn>
    </QuickGrid>
</div>
<Paginator State="@pagination"/>

@code {
    private QuickGrid<Country>? countriesGrid;
    PaginationState pagination = new PaginationState { ItemsPerPage = 10 };

    IQueryable<Country>? itemsQueryable = new List<Country>
    {
        new Country { Name = "USA", Medals = new Medals { Gold = 39, Silver
        = 41, Bronze = 33 } },
        new Country { Name = "China", Medals = new Medals { Gold = 38,
        Silver = 32, Bronze = 18 } },
        new Country { Name = "Japan", Medals = new Medals { Gold = 27,
        Silver = 14, Bronze = 17 } },
        new Country { Name = "Great Britain", Medals = new Medals { Gold =
        22, Silver = 21, Bronze = 22 } },
        new Country { Name = "Australia", Medals = new Medals { Gold = 17,
        Silver = 7, Bronze = 22 } },
        // Add more countries as needed
    }.AsQueryable();

    string nameFilter;
    int minMedals;
    int maxMedals = 120;
```

```
    IQueryable<Country> FilteredCountries
    {
        get
        {
            var result = itemsQueryable?.Where(c => c.Medals.Total <=
            maxMedals);

            if (!string.IsNullOrEmpty(nameFilter))
            {
                result = result.Where(c => c.Name.Contains(nameFilter,
                StringComparison.CurrentCultureIgnoreCase));
            }

            if (minMedals > 0)
            {
                result = result.Where(c => c.Medals.Total >= minMedals);
            }

            return result;
        }
    }

    public class Country
    {
        public string Name { get; set; }
        public Medals Medals { get; set; }
    }

    public class Medals
    {
        public int Gold { get; set; }
        public int Silver { get; set; }
        public int Bronze { get; set; }
        public int Total => Gold + Silver + Bronze;
    }
}
```

Look at a section of a `div` search box:

```
<input type="search" autofocus @bind="nameFilter"
    @bind:after="() => countriesGrid.HideColumnOptionsAsync()"
    placeholder="Country name..."/>
```

When the user types a country name and presses Enter, the options panel closes automatically, keeping the interface clean and intuitive.

For example, you could type:

☰ Name	Gold	Silver	Bronze	Total
		41	33	113
Great ✕		32	18	88
Japan	27	14	17	58
Great Britain	22	21	22	65
Australia	17	7	22	46

5 items |<   <   Page **1** of **1**   >   >|

After pressing Enter, you would get this:

☰ Name	Gold	Silver	Bronze	Total
Great Britain	22	21	22	65

1 items |<   <   Page **1** of **1**   >   >|

Reconnection UI Updates

Although the main objective of Blazor apps is to keep users connected and productive, occasionally server restarts or network outages are inevitable. Blazor's handling of these situations has been significantly improved in .NET 10, which benefits both developers and users. This section covers the changes, how to utilize the new features, and potential areas for personalization.

Introduction of the *ReconnectModal* Component

Blazor Web App templates now come with a new ReconnectModal component. This is a ready-to-use dialog that pops up when your app loses its connection to the server, like when your WiFi drops or the server restarts. Instead of leaving users confused, the app now shows a clear message and attempts to reconnect automatically.

What's really nice is that this modal isn't just a black box. It comes with its own styles and JavaScript, but you can fully customize how it looks and behaves. Want to add your company logo, change the wording, or update the colors? You can do all of that by editing the modal's markup and CSS right in your project.

What you need to do is simply add the new component called ReconnectModal. razor to your Layout directory using the following script:

```
<script type="module" src="@Assets["Components/Layout/ReconnectModal.razor.
js"]"></script>

<dialog id="components-reconnect-modal" data-nosnippet>
    <div class="components-reconnect-container">
        <div class="components-rejoining-animation" aria-hidden="true">
            <div></div>
            <div></div>
        </div>
        <p class="components-reconnect-first-attempt-visible">
            I've lost connection. Trying to rejoining the server...
        </p>
        <p class="components-reconnect-repeated-attempt-visible">
            Rejoin failed... trying again in <span
            id="components-seconds-to-next-attempt"></span> seconds.
        </p>
        <p class="components-reconnect-failed-visible">
            Failed to rejoin.<br/>Please retry or reload the page.
        </p>
        <button id="components-reconnect-button"
        class="components-reconnect-failed-visible">
            Retry
        </button>
        <p class="components-pause-visible">
```

```
        The session has been paused by the server.
    </p>
    <button id="components-resume-button"
    class="components-pause-visible">
        Resume
    </button>
    <p class="components-resume-failed-visible">
        Failed to resume the session.<br/>Please reload the page.
    </p>
    </div>
</dialog>
```

Without any changes in any other part of your solution, you will end up with a great modal whenever you lose connection to a server (see Figure 5-2).

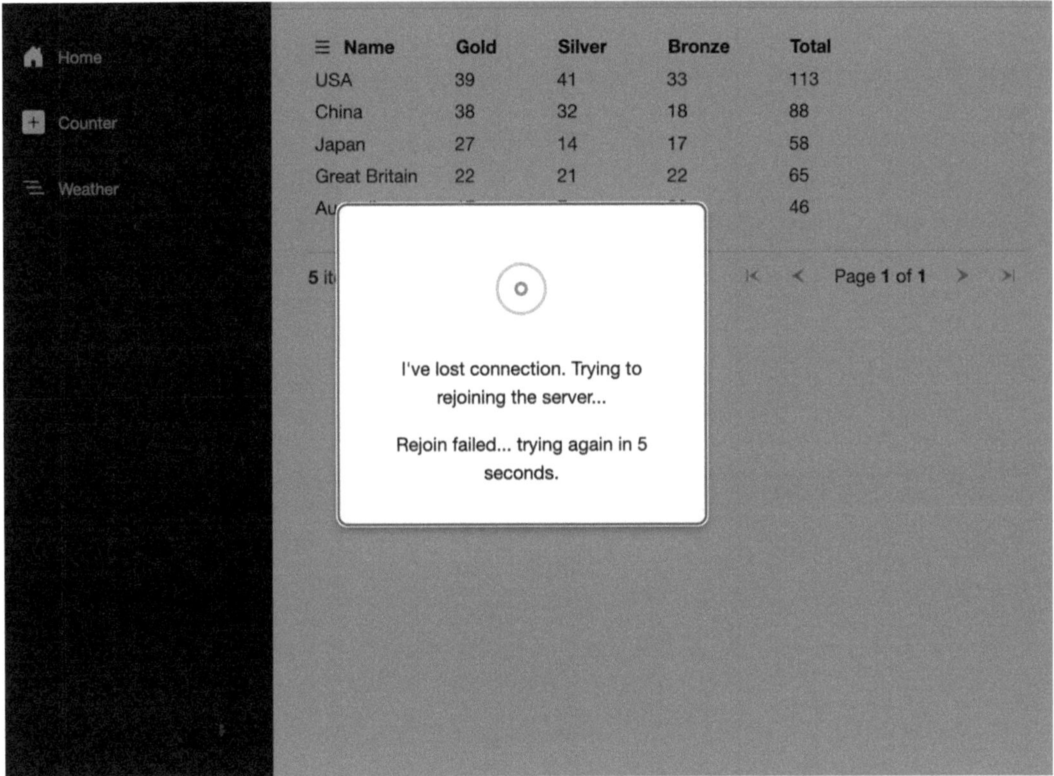

Figure 5-2. *The modal dialog showing that the connection has been lost*

CSP Compliance and Developer Customization

In the past, strict Content Security Policy (CSP) settings, particularly those that lock down inline styles, occasionally caused issues with Blazor's built-in reconnection user interface. This is resolved by the new ReconnectModal, which includes all styles in distinct files rather than injecting them programmatically. This indicates that your app can pass even the most rigorous CSP audits, which is crucial for government and business projects.

Customizing the modal is as simple as editing the CSS and HTML for the component. For example, you can delay how quickly the modal appears by updating your site's CSS:

```
#components-reconnect-modal {
    transition: visibility 0s linear 1000ms; /* Delay by 1 second */
}
```

New Reconnection States and Events

Additionally, more comprehensive reconnection states and events are introduced in .NET 10, which gives you more control and insight into what happens when the connection drops. The components-reconnect-show, components-reconnect-hide, components-reconnect-failed, and components-reconnect-rejected CSS classes are now used by the modal to indicate its state. This makes it simple to alter the look according to the situation.

Even more powerful is the new components-reconnect-state-changed event. You can listen for this event in your JavaScript and react to changes in the reconnection process. For example, you might want to log each attempt or trigger analytics:

```
const reconnectModal = document.getElementById("components-
reconnect-modal");

reconnectModal.addEventListener("components-reconnect-state-changed",
(event) => {
    if (event.detail.state === "show") {
        reconnectModal.showModal();
    } else if (event.detail.state === "hide") {
        reconnectModal.close();
    } else if (event.detail.state === "failed") {
```

```
    // Optionally, try to reconnect again
    Blazor.reconnect();
  } else if (event.detail.state === "rejected") {
    // The server refused the connection; reload the page
    location.reload();
  }
});
```

You can also display the current reconnect attempt and the maximum retries directly in your modal, making it clear to users what's happening:

```
<div id="components-reconnect-modal">
    There was a problem with the connection!
    (Current reconnect attempt: <span id="components-reconnect-current-
    attempt"></span>
    / <span id="components-reconnect-max-retries"></span>)
</div>
```

Why This Matters

These changes make Blazor apps feel more polished and intuitive when there are network outages. Security teams can relax knowing the app is CSP-compliant, and developers have more freedom and control. You have all the resources you require, regardless of your preference for simplicity or a branded reconnection user interface.

During development, simply try restarting your server or unplugging your network. You can modify the new modal to suit the needs and aesthetic of your app after seeing it in use. Blazor apps now feel even more streamlined and dependable thanks to this minor but significant update.

Declarative State Persistence

Blazor has always taken a somewhat balanced approach to state management. On the one hand, you want your app to feel quick and seamless even when users reload or switch between pages. However, you do not want to write a lot of boilerplate code in order to maintain a small number of values. Blazor offers a much more declarative and reliable method of preserving state between components, as well as between prerendering and interactive sessions, with .NET 10.

Declarative State Persistence: What's New?

In previous versions of Blazor, if you wanted to persist the state during prerendering (for example, to avoid reloading data when your app became interactive), you had to use the `PersistentComponentState` service directly. This meant writing extra code to check if the state was already available, register callbacks, and handle serialization. It worked, but it was easy to get lost in the details and clutter your components with logic that wasn't really about your app's core purpose.

Now, with .NET 10, you can handle this with a single attribute: `[SupplyParameterFromPersistentComponentState]`. Just decorate any property in your component with this attribute, and Blazor will automatically persist and restore its value as needed. This makes your components cleaner and lets you focus on what matters—your app's logic and user experience.

How It Works

Before the `[SupplyParameterFromPersistentComponentState]` attribute was introduced in .NET 10, persisting component state during prerendering in Blazor required a lot more manual effort and boilerplate code. You had to work directly with the `PersistentComponentState` service, handle serialization and deserialization yourself, and register callbacks to ensure state was saved and restored at the right times. This made the code harder to read and maintain, especially for beginners.

Here's what the old approach looked like in practice for a simple movie list page:

```
@page "/movies"
@implements IDisposable
@inject IMovieService MovieService
@inject PersistentComponentState ApplicationState

@if (MoviesList == null)
{
    <p><em>Loading...</em></p>
}
else
{
```

```
<QuickGrid Items="MoviesList">
    <!-- columns here -->
</QuickGrid>
}

@code {
    public List<Movie>? MoviesList { get; set; }
    private PersistingComponentStateSubscription? persistingSubscription;

    protected override async Task OnInitializedAsync()
    {
        // Try to restore state from the persistent component state
        if (!ApplicationState.TryTakeFromJson<List<Movie>>(nameof
        (MoviesList), out var movies))
        {
            MoviesList = await MovieService.GetMoviesAsync();
        }
        else
        {
            MoviesList = movies;
        }

        // Register a callback to persist the state before prerendering
        completes
        persistingSubscription = ApplicationState.
        RegisterOnPersisting(() =>
        {
            ApplicationState.PersistAsJson(nameof(MoviesList), MoviesList);
            return Task.CompletedTask;
        });
    }

    public void Dispose() => persistingSubscription?.Dispose();
}
```

In this code, you have to:

- Inject the `PersistentComponentState` service.

- Manually check if the state is available using `TryTakeFromJson`.

- Register a callback with `RegisterOnPersisting` to save the state before prerendering completes.

- Handle cleanup by implementing `IDisposable` and disposing the subscription.

This approach worked, but it was easy to make mistakes or forget a step, especially as your app grew more complex. The new declarative model in .NET 10, using just an attribute, is much simpler and less error-prone, letting you focus on your app's logic instead of plumbing code.

Now, your code can look as simple as this:

```
@page "/movies"
@inject IMovieService MovieService

@if (MoviesList == null)
{
    <p><em>Loading...</em></p>
}
else
{
    <QuickGrid Items="MoviesList">
        <!-- columns here -->
    </QuickGrid>
}

@code {
    [SupplyParameterFromPersistentComponentState]
    public List<Movie>? MoviesList { get; set; }

    protected override async Task OnInitializedAsync()
    {
        MoviesList ??= await MovieService.GetMoviesAsync();
    }
}
```

That's it! The `[SupplyParameterFromPersistentComponentState]` attribute tells Blazor to save the value of `MoviesList` when prerendering and to restore it automatically when the component is rendered interactively. No more manual subscriptions or custom serialization; Blazor takes care of it for you.

How Robust Is It?

Both components and services can benefit from this new strategy. Blazor uniquely identifies each piece of state for components by combining the property name, the component type, the parent component type, and an optional @key. This implies that if you supply unique keys when required (for instance, when rendering inside a loop), you can have multiple instances of the same component, each with its own state.

You can now register your service with the persistent state system if you want to keep state in your service (so it is accessible across the entire app). User preferences, shopping carts, and any other data that needs to withstand navigation and even reconnections can benefit from this.

Why Is This a Big Deal?

Less boilerplate code: You write less code and avoid the risk of forgetting to persist or restore state.

More reliable: The state is handled consistently across prerendering, navigation, and reconnection scenarios.

Declarative and clear: Your intent is obvious. Just mark what you want to keep, and Blazor does the rest.

Navigation and Routing Improvements

One of Blazor's strengths has always been its navigation and routing system, which provides developers with the means to create modern single-page web apps with fluid transitions and engaging content. Navigation is even more smooth, predictable, and developer-friendly in .NET 10 thanks to a number of well-considered enhancements. To fully benefit from these changes in your projects, this section examines them in more detail.

NavigateTo Behavior Changes: No More Scroll Jumps

In earlier versions of Blazor, using `NavigationManager.NavigateTo` to navigate to the same page would always scroll the browser viewport back to the top. This was fine for full page transitions, but it could be frustrating if you were updating just a part of the page, handling tab navigation, or working with anchor links. Users would lose their scroll position, leading to a jarring experience.

With .NET 10, this behavior has changed. Now, when you call `NavigateTo` for the current page (for example, to update a query string or fragment), Blazor no longer scrolls to the top. The page stays exactly where the user left it, making navigation feel much smoother, especially in apps with long pages or dynamic content.

How It Works

Suppose you have a page with a long list, and you want to update the query string to filter results without resetting the scroll:

```
@page "/products"
@inject NavigationManager Navigation

<button @onclick="() => Navigation.NavigateTo("/products?category=books")">
    Show Books
</button>
```

If you're already on `/products` and click the button, the page updates the URL and content, but the scroll position remains unchanged. This makes for a much more user-friendly experience.

If you still want to scroll to the top after navigation, you can do so manually with a bit of JavaScript:

```
javascript
window.scrollTo(0, 0);
```

Route Template Highlighting in Code Editors

Route template creation and upkeep can become challenging, particularly as your app expands. Hard-to-find bugs may result from typos or incorrectly placed parameters. Route template syntax highlighting in well-known editors like Visual Studio and VS Code is introduced in .NET 10. The editor now visually separates static segments, parameters, and constraints when you define a route in your controllers or components.

For example, in a route like /products/{id:int}, the {id:int} part is highlighted, making it obvious what's a parameter and what's static text. This helps you spot errors instantly and makes complex routes much easier to read and maintain.

Enhanced *NavLink* Matching

Blazor's NavLink component is the go-to way to create navigation links that automatically highlight when active. In .NET 10, its matching logic is smarter and more flexible:

- **Query strings and fragments are ignored:** When using NavLinkMatch.All, NavLink now ignores the query string and fragment parts of the URL. This means if your path matches but the query string or fragment changes, the link remains active. This is perfect for pages that use filters or tabs in the query string, keeping navigation cues consistent for users.

- **Custom matching logic:** If you need even more control, you can override the ShouldMatch method in a custom NavLink component. This lets you define exactly when a link should be considered active, maybe based on a combination of path, query, or custom rules.

Here's an example of a custom NavLink:

```
public class MyCustomNavLink : NavLink
{
    protected override bool ShouldMatch(string currentUriAbsolute)
    {
        // Only match if the path is exactly "/dashboard" and a specific
        query is present
        var uri = new Uri(currentUriAbsolute);
        return uri.AbsolutePath.Equals("/dashboard", StringComparison.
        OrdinalIgnoreCase)
                && uri.Query.Contains("tab=overview");
    }
}
```

This flexibility helps you build more dynamic navigation menus, especially in complex apps.

Improved Handling of "Not Found" Pages with the *NotFound* Method

Handling missing pages or invalid routes is a key part of any web app. .NET 10 introduces the `NavigationManager.NotFound` method, which makes it easier to show a proper "Not Found" page in both static server-side rendering (SSR) and interactive Blazor apps.

- **Static SSR:** Calling `NotFound` sets the HTTP status code to 404, so search engines and clients know the resource doesn't exist.

- **Interactive rendering:** The Blazor router now supports a `NotFoundPage` parameter, letting you specify a dedicated Razor component to render when a route isn't found.

Here's how you might set it up:

```
<Router AppAssembly="@typeof(Program).Assembly" NotFoundPage="typeof
(Pages.NotFound)">
    <Found Context="routeData">
        <RouteView RouteData="@routeData" />
    </Found>
    <NotFound>
        <!-- This will be ignored if NotFoundPage is set -->
    </NotFound>
</Router>
```

Now, whenever a user navigates to a nonexistent page, your custom `NotFound.razor` component is shown, providing a consistent and user-friendly experience.

Why These Changes Matter

Although these routing and navigation enhancements might not seem like much, they add up to a much more seamless and consistent user experience. Unexpected scroll jumps will not irritate your users; your navigation menus will function as you desire; and improved tooling and transparent error handling will make it simpler to write and maintain your code. These improvements will help you maintain your Blazor apps' stability, usability, and enjoyment as they expand.

Security and Authentication Updates

Building secure web apps has always required authentication, and with .NET 10, the process is much more streamlined and dependable, particularly when using Microsoft Entra ID (formerly Azure AD). If you have experience with authentication in previous versions, such as .NET 8, you will notice significant improvements in both the setup process and the behavior of your application at scale. It is also important to remember that these enhancements are not limited to Entra ID. Windows Authentication and OpenID Connect providers can now use the same simplified method.

The Old Way: .NET 9 and Its Challenges

Let's start with how things used to work. In .NET 8, you began by registering your app in the Azure portal and copying the necessary IDs and URIs into your `appsettings.json` file. You'd then set up authentication in your `Program.cs` file:

```
builder.Services.AddAuthentication(OpenIdConnectDefaults.
AuthenticationScheme)
    .AddMicrosoftIdentityWebApp(builder.Configuration.
GetSection("AzureAd"));
builder.Services.AddAuthorization();
```

This got you basic sign-in and sign-out, but if you needed to call a protected API say, Microsoft Graph, or your own backend, you had to manually request an access token and attach it to your HTTP requests. That meant injecting `ITokenAcquisition`, calling `GetAccessTokenForUserAsync`, and setting the `Authorization` header yourself:

```
var accessToken = await tokenAcquisition.GetAccessTokenForUserAsyn
c(scopes);
var client = httpClientFactory.CreateClient();
client.DefaultRequestHeaders.Authorization = new AuthenticationHeaderValue(
"Bearer", accessToken);
```

This approach worked, but it was repetitive and easy to get wrong. Things got even more complicated when you deployed your app to a web farm. The default in-memory token cache didn't work across multiple servers, so users could get logged out unexpectedly or see inconsistent behavior. To fix this, you had to set up a distributed cache and ensure your data protection keys were safely shared and encrypted, often a source of confusion and subtle bugs.

The New Way: .NET 10 Makes It Simple and Scalable

With .NET 10, the process feels much more natural. You still register your app and provide the configuration, but now you have the flexibility to use either `appsettings.json` or direct code configuration in `Program.cs`. The real magic comes in how you handle secure API calls and token caching.

Effortless Secure API Calls

Instead of manually handling tokens, .NET 10 lets you register a named HTTP client that automatically manages authentication for you. Here's how you set it up:

```
builder.Services.AddHttpClient("MyApi", client =>
{
    client.BaseAddress = new Uri("https://myapi.contoso.com/");
})
.AddHttpMessageHandler<MicrosoftIdentityUserAuthentication
MessageHandler>();
```

Now, when you need to call your API, you just inject the factory and use your named client:

```
public class MyApiService
{
    private readonly HttpClient _client;

    public MyApiService(IHttpClientFactory factory)
    {
        _client = factory.CreateClient("MyApi");
    }

    public async Task<IEnumerable<TodoItem>> GetTodosAsync()
    {
        var response = await _client.GetAsync("todos");
        response.EnsureSuccessStatusCode();
        return await response.Content.ReadFromJsonAsync<IEnumerable<Tod
oItem>>();
    }
}
```

The framework automatically fetches, attaches, and refreshes tokens as needed. You don't have to write any extra code for token management, which means fewer bugs and a more secure app.

Distributed Token Cache: Ready for the Real World

If your app runs on multiple servers, .NET 10 makes it much easier to keep everything in sync. You can set up a distributed cache, like Redis, SQL Server, or Azure Cosmos DB, with just a few lines of configuration. Here's an example using Redis:

```
builder.Services.AddStackExchangeRedisCache(options =>
{
    options.Configuration = builder.Configuration.
GetConnectionString("Redis");
    options.InstanceName = "MyApp:";
});

builder.Services.AddDataProtection()
    .PersistKeysToAzureBlobStorage("<blob-uri>")
    .ProtectKeysWithAzureKeyVault("<key-vault-uri>", new
    DefaultAzureCredential());

builder.Services.AddAuthentication(OpenIdConnectDefaults.
AuthenticationScheme)
    .AddMicrosoftIdentityWebApp(builder.Configuration.
    GetSection("AzureAd"))
    .EnableTokenAcquisitionToCallDownstreamApi()
    .AddDistributedTokenCaches();
```

Now, all your servers share a single, encrypted token cache, and your data protection keys are safely stored and protected in Azure. You don't have to worry about users being logged out when their requests hit different servers, and you can scale your app confidently.

OpenID Connect and Windows Auth Considerations

One of the best parts about these improvements is that they're not limited to Microsoft Entra ID. If you're using another OpenID Connect provider, like Auth0, Okta, or Google, the process is nearly identical. You configure your provider, set up your named HTTP clients, and let the framework handle the rest. The same goes for Windows Authentication in internal apps: distributed token caching and secure API calls work just as smoothly, making it easy to build secure, scalable solutions for any scenario.

Why This Matters

Authentication is a breeze with .NET 10. Your apps are safer, you write less code, and moving to a web farm is no longer a hassle. The security story is much stronger, and the configuration is flexible. You get the same straightforward, reliable experience whether you are using Windows Auth, Entra ID, or another OpenID Connect provider.

You will value how .NET 10 allows you to concentrate on developing your application rather than battling your infrastructure if you have ever had trouble with manual token management, perplexing cache configurations, or enigmatic authentication issues. Blazor Web Apps has advanced significantly with this release, offering enterprise-grade security and scalability to all users immediately.

Interactivity and Real-Time Features

Real-time features are a huge part of what makes modern web apps feel alive and responsive. In .NET 10, Blazor and ASP.NET Core have taken a big step forward by adding native support for Server-Sent Events (SSEs). This makes it much easier to stream data from your server to your users as it happens, opening the door to new interactive experiences without all the heavy lifting that used to be required.

Native Support for Server-Sent Events (SSE)

Server-Sent Events (SSEs) is a web standard that lets your server push updates to the browser over a single, long-lived HTTP connection. Unlike polling, where the client keeps asking the server for updates, SSE lets the server send new data whenever it's available. This is perfect for things like live dashboards, notifications, stock tickers, or even collaborative tools where users need to see updates in real time.

In the past, if you wanted to use SSE in a .NET app, you had to write a lot of boilerplate code. You needed to manually set HTTP headers, keep the connection open, and write each event to the response stream yourself. It worked, but it wasn't pretty, and it was easy to get wrong.

Now, with .NET 10, SSE is a first-class citizen. You can return a stream of events from your endpoint using a simple, strongly-typed API. You simply create an IAsyncEnumerable<T> that yields your event data, and then you return it using the new ServerSentEvents result type in your minimal API or controller.

Example: Streaming Orders in Real Time

Imagine you're building a food ordering app and want to show new orders as they come in. Here's how you might set up an SSE endpoint:

```csharp
public record OrderEvent(string OrderId, string Food, DateTime PlacedAt);

public static async IAsyncEnumerable<OrderEvent> GetOrderEvents([Enumerator
Cancellation] CancellationToken cancellationToken)
{
    while (!cancellationToken.IsCancellationRequested)
    {
        // Simulate a new order every 2 seconds
        await Task.Delay(2000, cancellationToken);
        yield return new OrderEvent(Guid.NewGuid().ToString(), "🍕 Pizza",

        DateTime.UtcNow);
    }
}

// In your Program.cs or endpoint setup
app.MapGet("/orders", (CancellationToken token) =>
    TypedResults.ServerSentEvents(GetOrderEvents(token), eventType:
    "order")
);
```

On the client side, you can use the standard JavaScript `EventSource` API to receive these updates:

```javascript
const source = new EventSource('/orders');
source.onmessage = function(event) {
    const order = JSON.parse(event.data);
    console.log('New order:', order);
    // Update your UI here
};
```

Use Cases and Scenarios

SSE is a great fit for any scenario where you want to push updates from the server to many clients at once, and you don't need the client to send messages back over the same connection. Some classic examples include:

- Live news feeds

- Monitoring dashboards (CPU usage, server health, IoT data)

- Notifications and alerts

- Collaborative editing (showing who's online or typing)

- Stock tickers or auction updates

Because SSE uses plain HTTP, it works well with proxies and firewalls, and it's simpler to scale than some other real-time technologies.

How SSE Compares to SignalR

If you've used Blazor or ASP.NET Core before, you might be familiar with SignalR. SignalR is Microsoft's abstraction for real-time web communication. It can use WebSockets, long polling, or SSE under the hood, and it supports two-way communication. The server can push updates to the client, and the client can send messages back to the server.

So, when should you use SSE and when should you use SignalR?

- **SSE is best when you only need server-to-client updates:** It's lighter, uses less bandwidth, and is easier to implement for simple streaming scenarios. If you're building a live feed or dashboard where the client just needs to listen, SSE is a perfect fit.

- **SignalR is better for full-duplex (two-way) communication:** If your app needs to send messages from the client to the server as well as from the server to the client—think chat apps or games—SignalR is the way to go. It also handles connection management and fallback strategies for you.

With .NET 10, you can choose the right tool for the job without extra complexity. For many real-time needs, SSE is now as simple as writing a few lines of code. For more interactive scenarios, SignalR still has you covered.

Migration and Compatibility Considerations

There are some significant changes that will impact the way your Blazor application is constructed, served, and functions in the browser when you update it to .NET 10. As with any significant update, there are some migration and compatibility issues to be aware of, but these changes are intended to make your apps faster, more dependable, and easier to maintain. This section explains what is new, what to look out for, and how to deal with any unexpected changes that may arise.

Serving Blazor Scripts as Static Assets: Migration Considerations

One of the most impactful changes in .NET 10 is how Blazor scripts are served as static web assets. In previous versions, core Blazor JavaScript files like `blazor.web.js` or `blazor.webassembly.js` were embedded resources, delivered from the ASP.NET Core shared framework. This meant they didn't benefit from the same optimizations as your other static files, such as automatic compression and fingerprinting.

With .NET 10, these scripts are now published as static assets alongside your app. This brings big advantages: the files are automatically compressed and fingerprinted, which means smaller downloads and better caching for your users. But it also means you need to be aware of how your hosting environment serves static files. For most projects, this transition is seamless. However, if you have custom middleware or restrictive static file settings, you'll want to double-check that the new script files are being served correctly. If you deploy to environments where static files are handled separately (like certain cloud platforms or CDNs), make sure your deployment scripts pick up these new assets.

If you notice that your app fails to load or the browser can't find the Blazor script, check your published output for the new script files and verify that your server is configured to serve them. This is especially important if you're using custom build or deployment pipelines.

AppContext Switches for Legacy Navigation Behavior

Another subtle but important change in .NET 10 is how Blazor handles navigation events. In earlier versions, calling NavigateTo with the same URL would always scroll the page to the top, even if you were just updating a query string or fragment. This behavior has changed: now, navigating to the same page no longer resets the scroll position, resulting in a smoother user experience.

If your app relies on the old behavior, perhaps you want to force a scroll to the top on every navigation, you can restore it using an AppContext switch. Add the following to your project's runtime configuration file (runtimeconfig.json):

```
{
  "runtimeOptions": {
    "configProperties": {
      "Microsoft.AspNetCore.Components.Web.
      BrowserScrollToTopOnNavigate": true
    }
  }
}
```

This gives you full control over navigation behavior, so you can choose what works best for your users and your app's design.

Breaking Changes and How to Address Them

Every major release brings a few breaking changes, and .NET 10 is no exception. The most common issues you might encounter when migrating a Blazor app include these:

- **Script loading errors:** If your app or hosting environment doesn't serve the new static Blazor script files correctly, your app may fail to start. Check your static file settings and deployment scripts and ensure that the new files are present and accessible.

- **Custom JavaScript interop:** If you have custom JavaScript that references Blazor's bootstrapping scripts by their old names or locations, update those references to point to the new static asset paths.

- **Navigation differences:** As mentioned, the default navigation behavior has changed. If your app depends on scrolling to the top after navigation, use the `AppContext` switch to restore the old behavior.

- **Third-party libraries:** Some libraries or components may assume the old script loading or navigation behaviors. Make sure you're using the latest versions of any dependencies and check their documentation for .NET 10 compatibility notes.

The best way to spot and address breaking changes is to test your app thoroughly after upgrading. Pay special attention to startup, navigation, and any custom JavaScript integrations. If you run into issues, consult the .NET 10 migration guides and release notes for detailed troubleshooting steps.

Making the Most of .NET 10

Even though these migration procedures may seem like extra work, they actually improve caching, speed up app startup, and improve user experience. You will be in a good position to benefit from all that Blazor in .NET 10 has to offer if you take the time to check your static file setup, adjust navigation settings as necessary, and test your app after upgrading.

Keep in mind that every new release offers an opportunity to improve your app, not just by adding new features, but also by eliminating outdated workarounds and ensuring that your codebase is future-ready. Those enhancements are well worth the work with .NET 10.

Best Practices and Real-World Scenarios

As you bring Blazor's new features into a real-world production environment, it's not just about knowing what's possible, it's about knowing how to use these tools to build robust, maintainable, and delightful applications. This section looks at some best practices for leveraging the latest Blazor capabilities, explores practical scenarios where these features shine, and highlights a few common pitfalls so you can avoid them from day one.

Tips for Leveraging New Blazor Features in Production

Start by utilizing the latest performance enhancements when getting ready to install or update a Blazor app. For instance, serving Blazor scripts as static assets has a direct impact on how quickly users can load your app and is not merely a technical detail. Make sure these assets are published and served correctly by your deployment process, particularly if you are using a CDN or a custom hosting setup. Verify that all scripts and resources load without hiccups and that caching is operating as it should by testing your application in a production-like setting.

Spend some time utilizing the new tracing and diagnostic tools included in .NET 10. It used to be nearly impossible to find memory leaks or performance issues in Blazor WebAssembly. You can now gather memory dumps and traces directly from the browser, providing you with tangible information to help improve your application. Make it a practice to profile your app before and during development. This will enable you to identify problems long before your users do.

Adopt the new declarative state persistence for state management. Use the `[SupplyParameterFromPersistentComponentState]` attribute to save and restore the component state rather than writing custom code. This maintains the cleanliness of your components and guarantees a consistent experience, particularly when prerendering or reconnecting following a network outage.

Pay attention to the new default behaviors in routing and navigation. For instance, Blazor's default same-page navigation no longer scrolls to the top. Use the provided `AppContext` switches to change it if your users are expecting a different behavior. Test navigation flows frequently, particularly in applications that handle complex query strings or deep linking.

Sample Use Cases: Dashboards, Admin Panels, and Real-Time Apps

Blazor's improvements really shine in data-rich applications. Imagine you're building a dashboard for a logistics company. With the enhanced `QuickGrid` component, you can display thousands of rows with dynamic styling, overdue shipments in red, completed deliveries in green, and everything else styled based on business rules. The new `RowClass` parameter makes this kind of visual feedback almost effortless.

For admin panels, the improved navigation and state persistence mean users can move between sections, filter data, and even lose connection without losing their place or their work. The new reconnection UI ensures that users always know what's happening if the network hiccups, and the modal is easy to customize to match your brand.

If you're building a real-time app, say, a live monitoring tool for factory sensors, native Server-Sent Events (SSEs) support lets you stream updates directly to the browser with minimal overhead. You can push temperature changes, alerts, or production stats as they happen, and users see updates instantly. For two-way communication, like chat or collaborative editing, SignalR is still your go-to, but for one-way streaming, SSE is now a breeze.

Common Pitfalls and How to Avoid Them

One of the most common mistakes when upgrading to .NET 10 is overlooking static asset configuration. If your scripts aren't loading, double-check your static file settings and deployment scripts. Make sure you're not accidentally blocking or omitting the new Blazor script files.

Another pitfall is assuming that navigation will work exactly as before. The new default behavior for `NavigateTo` can surprise you if you're relying on scroll resets or other legacy quirks. Test your navigation thoroughly and use the `AppContext` switch if you need to restore the old behavior.

For state management, don't mix manual and declarative approaches unless you have a very specific reason. The new attribute-based persistence is reliable and much easier to maintain; embrace it fully for a smoother development experience.

Finally, don't forget about security and distributed token caching if you're deploying to a web farm or using authentication. With .NET 10, it's easier than ever to set up, but skipping this step can lead to confusing bugs and user complaints about unexpected sign-outs.

Bringing It All Together

The best way to master these new Blazor features is to use them in real, meaningful projects. Whether you're building a dashboard, an admin tool, or a live data app, the improvements in .NET 10 will help you deliver a faster, more reliable, and more enjoyable user experience. Test thoroughly, embrace the declarative tools, and keep your deployment pipeline up to date with the latest best practices. With these habits, you'll get the most out of Blazor and your users will notice the difference.

CHAPTER 6

Unlocking .NET MAUI's Potential

Introduction

When developers consider building apps that run smoothly on multiple platforms, whether it's Windows, macOS, Android, or iOS, .NET *MAUI* (*multi-platform app UI*) stands out as a powerful and flexible framework. It's the evolution of *Xamarin.Forms,* designed to simplify cross-platform development by letting you write your app's code once and run it anywhere. Over the years, .NET MAUI has grown from a promising idea into a mature toolkit that helps developers create beautiful, responsive, and high-performing apps with less hassle.

With the release of .NET 10, .NET MAUI takes another big step forward. This latest version isn't just about adding new features. It's about refining the experience for developers and users alike. The focus is clear: improve quality, boost performance, and make the developer's life easier. These goals shape every change and enhancement in .NET MAUI for .NET 10, ensuring that apps built with it are faster, more reliable, and more enjoyable to create.

So, what exactly has changed? The updates in .NET 10 cover a broad range of areas, from simplifying how you write XAML, the markup language used for designing UI, to modernizing animation APIs and improving platform-specific features. Some controls have been enhanced or replaced, making it easier to build rich interfaces. Performance improvements mean your apps start faster and run smoother. And there's a stronger emphasis on integrating with modern tools and libraries, helping you tap into a vibrant community ecosystem.

© Kajetan Duszyński 2025
K. Duszyński, *.NET 10 Revealed,* https://doi.org/10.1007/979-8-8688-1889-9_6

All these changes matter because they directly impact how quickly you can build apps and how well those apps perform in the real world. Whether you're starting a new project or upgrading an existing one, .NET MAUI in .NET 10 offers a more polished, productive, and enjoyable development journey. This chapter guides you through these updates step by step, showing you practical examples and explaining why each improvement is worth knowing about. You'll explore how .NET MAUI is shaping the future of cross-platform app development.

Getting Started with .NET MAUI in .NET 10

Setting Up a New MAUI Project Targeting .NET 10

Starting a new .NET MAUI project with .NET 10 is straightforward and gives you access to the latest features and improvements. First, make sure you have the .NET 10 SDK installed on your machine. You can download it from the official .NET website. If you are using Visual Studio, ensure that it's updated to the latest version that supports .NET 10 and the MAUI workload.

To create a new project in Visual Studio, follow these steps:

1. Open Visual Studio and select Create a New Project.

2. In the project templates, search for MAUI, and choose .NET MAUI App.

3. Click Next, name your project, and choose a location.

4. In the next window, select .NET 10 as the target framework.

5. Click Create and wait for Visual Studio to scaffold your new project and restore dependencies.

If you prefer the command line, you can use the following command to create a new MAUI app targeting .NET 10:

```
dotnet new mauiapp -o MyApp -f net10.0
```

This command creates a new folder called MyApp with a .NET MAUI project set up for .NET 10. You can now open this folder in Visual Studio or Visual Studio Code and start developing your cross-platform app.

Upgrading Existing MAUI Projects

Upgrading your existing .NET MAUI project to .NET 10 is a great way to benefit from the latest performance, quality, and tooling enhancements. Here's how you can do it:

1. Update the target framework: Open your project's `.csproj` file and change the `TargetFrameworks` property to use `net10.0` for each platform you target. For example:

   ```
   <TargetFrameworks>net10.0-android;net10.0-ios;net10.0-
   maccatalyst;net10.0-windows10.0.19041.0</TargetFrameworks>
   ```

2. Update MAUI NuGet packages: .NET MAUI in .NET 10 is delivered as a set of NuGet packages. Update all `Microsoft.Maui.*` package references to the latest versions compatible with .NET 10. You can do this in Visual Studio's NuGet Package Manager or by editing the `.csproj` file directly.

3. Update the MAUI workload: Run the following command to ensure you have the latest MAUI workload installed:

   ```
   dotnet workload update
   ```

4. Clean and rebuild: Delete the `bin` and `obj` folders in your project directory to remove old build artifacts, then rebuild your project.

5. Review and adjust the code: Check for any deprecated APIs or breaking changes introduced in .NET 10. Update your code as needed, following the migration guides and release notes.

6. Test on all platforms: Run your app on each target platform (Android, iOS, Windows, macOS) to confirm everything works as expected

.NET MAUI Workload and NuGet Package Updates

.NET MAUI is distributed as both a .NET workload and a set of NuGet packages. Here's what you need to know:

- **Workload:** The MAUI workload provides the tools and templates for building MAUI apps. You install or update it using the CLI:

  ```
  dotnet workload install maui
  dotnet workload update
  ```

- Keeping the workload up to date ensures you have the latest project templates, build tools, and platform support.

- **NuGet packages:** Your MAUI project references several `Microsoft.Maui.*` NuGet packages. These packages are versioned separately from the SDK and workload, allowing you to pin your project to specific versions or try preview builds. You can update these packages in Visual Studio or via the CLI:

  ```
  dotnet add package Microsoft.Maui.Controls --version 10.*
  ```

Best Practices

Always keep your workload and NuGet packages in sync with your target .NET SDK version.

When a new version of .NET is released, update both the SDK and the corresponding MAUI workload and NuGet packages.

For multi-project solutions, consider defining the `MauiVersion` property in a shared file like `Directory.Packages.props` to keep versions consistent.

By following these steps, you'll be ready to build, upgrade, and maintain .NET MAUI apps using all the new capabilities of .NET 10. The process is designed to be as smooth as possible, letting you focus on building great cross-platform applications.

XAML Improvements and Simplification in .NET MAUI 10

Working with XAML in .NET MAUI has always made it easy to see and manage your user interface. With .NET 10, things just got simpler and cleaner. The changes are focused on saving time, reducing confusion, and making your files much easier to read.

Global and Implicit XML Namespaces in XAML

Previously, every XAML file needed several `xmlns` lines at the top. You would have to keep track of which namespaces you were using and sometimes create unique prefixes. This often led to mistakes or copy-pasting long boilerplate code from file to file.

Now, in .NET 10, you can use a global XML namespace. With this, you register all the namespaces your project uses in one place. Your XAML files can then use those types and controls directly, without needing to declare the same namespace in every file. Even better, if you opt in to implicit namespaces, you can skip declaring most namespaces altogether. The system knows what's available, and your files stay tidy.

For example, here's how a `ContentPage` used to look:

```
<ContentPage
    xmlns="http://schemas.microsoft.com/dotnet/2021/maui"
    xmlns:x="http://schemas.microsoft.com/winfx/2009/xaml"
    xmlns:models="clr-namespace:MyApp.Models"
    xmlns:controls="clr-namespace:MyApp.Controls"
    x:Class="MyApp.MainPage">
    <controls:TagView x:DataType="models:Tag" />
</ContentPage>
```

With global namespaces, the same page now looks like this:

```
<ContentPage
    xmlns="http://schemas.microsoft.com/dotnet/maui/global"
    xmlns:x="http://schemas.microsoft.com/winfx/2009/xaml"
    x:Class="MyApp.MainPage">
    <TagView x:DataType="Tag" />
</ContentPage>
```

And if you opt in to implicit namespaces, you can make it even cleaner:

```
<ContentPage x:Class="MyApp.MainPage">
    <TagView x:DataType="Tag" />
</ContentPage>
```

No more long lists of `xmlns` declarations. Everything you need is set up globally and ready to use.

Cleaner XAML Files: Removing Boilerplate Code

The main benefit is clear: your XAML files are much shorter and easier to understand. You won't waste time scrolling past or editing old namespace lines. When you add third-party controls, you only need to register their namespace once, not in every single file.

If you ever run into situations where you have two things with the same name, you can still add a prefix for just that case. So, you get all the benefits of simplicity without losing any options.

Adopting New XAML Features in Existing Projects

If you're starting a new MAUI project in .NET 10, these features are ready right out of the box. To use them in an existing project, follow these steps:

1. Upgrade your project to target .NET 10.

2. Add a global namespace mapping by creating a `GlobalXmlns.cs` file in your project. For each namespace you want available globally, add a line like this:

   ```
   [assembly: XmlnsDefinition("http://schemas.microsoft.com/
   dotnet/maui/global", "MyApp.Controls")]
   ```

3. Enable implicit namespaces in your `.csproj` file by including this:

   ```
   <PropertyGroup>
     <DefineConstants>$(DefineConstants);MauiAllowImplicitXmlns
     Declaration</DefineConstants>
     <EnablePreviewFeatures>true</EnablePreviewFeatures>
   </PropertyGroup>
   ```

4. Remove redundant namespace declarations from your XAML files. Just use your controls directly or add a prefix if you have naming conflicts.

5. Test your project. IntelliSense and Hot Reload continue to work as expected, and your code will look a lot cleaner.

These changes make it easier to maintain big projects. You spend less time managing the top of your XAML files and focus more on building features.

.NET Aspire Integration

Imagine building a modern app where your mobile frontend connects naturally to multiple services, APIs, databases, or even background tasks, while handling tricky parts like scaling, monitoring, health checks, and keeping configuration up to date. That's where .NET Aspire steps in, and it's changing the game for .NET MAUI developers.

What Is .NET Aspire and Why It Matters for MAUI

.NET Aspire is a set of tools, templates, and NuGet packages that make app development in distributed and cloud-ready environments much smoother. It helps connect your app to different backend services and makes your solution more robust by automating a lot of common setup: things like telemetry (think logging, metrics, and tracing), service discovery (letting pieces of your app find each other automatically), and configuration management (making sure config values are always correct across different environments).

For .NET MAUI developers, .NET Aspire changes the game by providing a common approach to working with services regardless of the platform your app runs on. It automatically sets up crucial production features behind the scenes, including health checks, robust logging, and distributed tracing, all of which used to require significant manual work. As a result, every app you build is more stable, better monitored, and ready for real-world scaling and troubleshooting.

Using the New .NET Aspire Project Template

Getting started with Aspire in your MAUI app is simple thanks to new project templates. You can create a solution that already links your MAUI frontend, API backends, and all the orchestration in between.

Here's a typical workflow:

1. Create the solution from a template:

    In Visual Studio, just search for Aspire in the new project window and select the MAUI + Aspire template, or use:

    ```
    dotnet new maui-aspire -o MyApp
    ```

    This sets up the scaffold. You'll get an `AppHost` project (to coordinate everything), a `ServiceDefaults` project (with ready-to-use configs for resilience and telemetry), and your MAUI app wired to benefit from all Aspire's features.

2. Link your app to Aspire services:

    In your MAUI project's `MauiProgram.cs` file, call this:

    ```
    builder.AddServiceDefaults();
    ```

    This one line brings in all the "smarts" from Aspire: telemetry, service discovery, health checks, and full integration with distributed app features.

3. Customize the experience:

    Do you need to reference another service, like your backend API? Update the distributed application builder in your `HostApp` project to add references:

    ```
    var builder = DistributedApplication.CreateBuilder(args);
    var webapi = builder.AddProject<Projects.Api>("api");
    builder.AddProject<Projects.MauiApp>("mauiapp").
    WithReference(webapi);
    builder.Build().Run();
    ```

This ensures your MAUI frontend discovers and speaks to backend services seamlessly.

Telemetry, Service Discovery, and Configuration for Mobile Apps

A key benefit is Aspire's built-in telemetry. `OpenTelemetry` support comes standard, so your logs, metrics, and traces are collected with no extra configuration. Errors, slow responses, or dependency hiccups can all be monitored from Aspire's dashboard, offering real-time visibility into your app's health from development to production.

Service discovery is no longer a hassle, thanks to Aspire's automatic endpoint management. Instead of hard-coding URLs or worrying about different addresses for test, development, and production, Aspire resolves all service connections at runtime safely across any environment.

Configuration management is improved, too. All settings, connection strings, and feature flags are centrally managed, with Aspire separating configurations based on the environment. Injecting secrets or adjusting API endpoints for a specific platform is now reliable and quick, so you can move between environments without fear of mismatches or leaks.

Here's a simplified example in `MauiProgram.cs` for telemetry and service defaults:

```
public static MauiApp CreateMauiApp()
{
    var builder = MauiApp.CreateBuilder();
    builder
        .UseMauiApp<App>()
        .AddServiceDefaults();

    return builder.Build();
}
```

This works across platforms, no matter if you're on Android, iOS, Windows, or Mac.

Control Enhancements and Deprecations

When you build a user interface, every detail in how controls behave and look shapes the way people feel about your app. With .NET MAUI in .NET 10, Microsoft has taken a big step to make controls more powerful, more customizable, and easier to use for developers at all stages of experience. This section brings together the most important upgrades, each paired with a simple example, and suggests just where a screenshot from your app would best highlight what's new.

CollectionView and *CarouselView*

`CollectionView` is now the main handler for presenting lists or collections of data. Formerly, developers leaned on `ListView`, but `CollectionView` includes:

- **Better performance:** It has more efficient data virtualization, reducing memory usage and boosting scrolling speed, especially for large datasets.

- **Improved layouts:** You can easily switch between vertical lists, horizontal scrolls, and custom grid arrangements without extra templates.

- **Simplified handling:** With the new default, you don't need workarounds for grouping or custom cells.

Example

```
<!-- Collection View -->
    <CollectionView
        Grid.Row="1"
        ItemsSource="{Binding Items}"
        BackgroundColor="Transparent">

        <CollectionView.ItemTemplate>
            <DataTemplate>
                <Border Style="{StaticResource CardBorder}">
                    <Grid>
                        <Grid.ColumnDefinitions>
                            <ColumnDefinition Width="60" />
                            <ColumnDefinition Width="*" />
                            <ColumnDefinition Width="Auto" />
                        </Grid.ColumnDefinitions>
                        <Grid.RowDefinitions>
                            <RowDefinition Height="Auto" />
                            <RowDefinition Height="Auto" />
                        </Grid.RowDefinitions>
```

```xml
            <!-- Icon -->
            <Label
                Grid.Column="0"
                Grid.RowSpan="2"
                Text="{Binding Icon}"
                Style="{StaticResource IconStyle}" />

            <!-- Product Info -->
            <StackLayout Grid.Column="1" Grid.RowSpan="2"
            Spacing="6">
                <Label
                    Text="{Binding Name}"
                    Style="{StaticResource TitleStyle}" />
                <Label
                    Text="{Binding Description}"
                    Style="{StaticResource
                    DescriptionStyle}" />
            </StackLayout>

            <!-- Category Badge -->
            <Label
                Grid.Column="2"
                Grid.Row="0"
                Text="{Binding Category}"
                Style="{StaticResource CategoryStyle}"
                VerticalOptions="Start"
                HorizontalOptions="End" />
        </Grid>
    </Border>
</DataTemplate>
</CollectionView.ItemTemplate>

<!-- Empty View -->
<CollectionView.EmptyView>
    <StackLayout HorizontalOptions="Center"
    VerticalOptions="Center">
        <Label
```

```
                    Text="No products available"
                    FontSize="18"
                    TextColor="#95A5A6"
                    HorizontalOptions="Center" />
            </StackLayout>
        </CollectionView.EmptyView>

    </CollectionView>
```

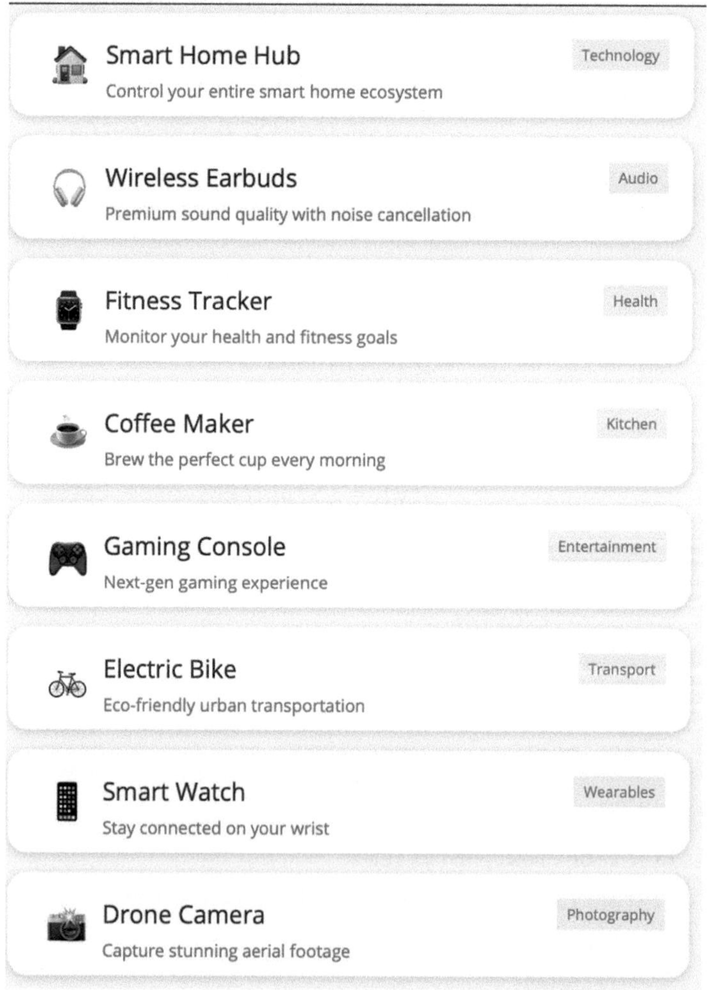

`CarouselView` enjoys similar handler-level upgrades:

- **Faster rendering:** Swiping through images or cards is noticeably smoother.

- **Native experience:** Gestures feel more natural across platforms with standardized paging and snapping.

Example

```
<CarouselView
        Grid.Row="1"
        ItemsSource="{Binding ImageItems}"
        Position="{Binding CurrentPosition, Mode=TwoWay}"
        BackgroundColor="Transparent"
        PeekAreaInsets="40">

        <CarouselView.ItemTemplate>
            <DataTemplate>
                <Grid Padding="10">
                    <Border
                        StrokeThickness="0"
                        StrokeShape="RoundRectangle 16"
                        BackgroundColor="Transparent">
                        <Image
                            Source="{Binding Url}"
                            Aspect="AspectFill"
                            HeightRequest="400" />
                    </Border>
                </Grid>
            </DataTemplate>
        </CarouselView.ItemTemplate>
    </CarouselView>
```

Entry and Editor: Android Feels Native

For Android, the Entry and Editor controls now tap into new native handlers. This includes:

- **Snappier keyboard and cursor:** The soft keyboard pops up correctly and respects input type (like numeric or password). Text selection and movement are much smoother, making the app feel more at home on Android.

- **Accessibility:** Better support for accessibility actions, meaning apps are easier to use for everyone.

Example:

```
<VerticalStackLayout Padding="12">
  <Entry Placeholder="Enter your username"/>
  <Editor Placeholder="Type your message here..." MaxLength="160"/>
</VerticalStackLayout>
```

HybridWebView: New Ways to Interact with Web Content

The HybridWebView has been updated to bridge the gap between web and native content by letting you call JavaScript functions directly from your C# code, and now even fetch typed results back to .NET. This allows you to integrate dynamic web content, like dashboards or custom widgets, much faster, with less glue code and far fewer errors. These enhancements also deliver a performance boost and remove a lot of lower-level complexity when working with mixed content.

Example

```
string result = await hybridWebView.EvaluateJavaScriptAsync<string>
("getStatus()");
```

New Capabilities of Switch and SearchBar

Customization capabilities have grown as well, especially for SearchBar and Switch. You can now control the color of the Cancel button in SearchBar, ensuring it matches your application's theme. Improved event handling for text change makes searching or filtering lists more dynamic and responsive. For Switch, the addition of the OffColor property means the control can visually communicate its state even more effectively. Setting distinct colors for both "on" and "off" positions not only fits your brand but also makes toggles easier to understand, helping users avoid confusion.

Example

```
<Switch OnColor="Orange" OffColor="DarkGray"/>
```

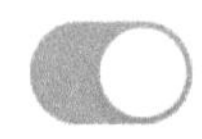

Finally, the thriving MAUI community brings fresh options like ColorPicker and DockLayout through well-supported third-party libraries. ColorPicker adds a native color-picking dialog so users can easily choose colors, which is handy for design or personalization features. DockLayout, meanwhile, gives you a powerful way to align controls along the sides of a container, cutting down on the amount of XAML you must write to produce complex or responsive layouts. These controls are designed to work consistently across platforms, so apps behave predictably for everyone.

Colorpicker:

```
<toolkit:ColorPicker SelectedColor="{Binding SelectedColor}" />
```

DockLayout:

```
<toolkit:DockLayout>
  <Button Text="Left" toolkit:DockLayout.Dock="Left"/>
  <Label Text="Center"/>
</toolkit:DockLayout>
```

Each of these enhancements is focused on making app building friendlier, reducing friction, and giving you more flexibility to deliver modern, engaging user experiences without overcomplicating your codebase. Whether you're updating old projects or starting something new, these changes will save time, prevent bugs, and let your creativity shine through clearer than ever before.

Deprecated Controls and Migration

As .NET MAUI evolves, some familiar controls from *Xamarin.Forms*—like ListView, TableView, and several "cell" types—are now deprecated. This means you shouldn't use them for new projects, and you'll want to replace them in existing code to benefit from improved performance and future compatibility.

Why Are ListView, TableView, and Related Cells Deprecated?

- ListView and TableView served well for displaying lists and tables, but they struggled with performance, especially for large or dynamic collections. They required more manual work to support templates, grouping, and custom layouts.

- Cells such as TextCell, ImageCell, and SwitchCell depended on these containers, making customization and cross-platform consistency harder to guarantee.

- .NET MAUI now offers CollectionView and CarouselView as their modern replacements. These controls offer better rendering speed, more flexible layouts, and simpler data binding, helping you create responsive UIs with less code.

Migration Strategies

Moving away from deprecated controls may sound daunting, but the migration path is clear and manageable. Here's how to update your projects:

1. Replace ListView with CollectionView.

   ListView was often used to show lists of simple or complex items. In most scenarios, you can directly replace ListView with CollectionView:

   Before (ListView):

```
<ListView ItemsSource="{Binding Items}">
  <ListView.ItemTemplate>
    <DataTemplate>
      <TextCell Text="{Binding Name}" Detail="{Binding Info}" />
    </DataTemplate>
  </ListView.ItemTemplate>
</ListView>
```

   After (CollectionView):

```
<CollectionView ItemsSource="{Binding Items}">
```

```
<CollectionView.ItemTemplate>
  <DataTemplate>
    <VerticalStackLayout Padding="10">
      <Label Text="{Binding Name}" FontSize="18"/>
      <Label Text="{Binding Info}" FontSize="14"
      TextColor="Gray"/>
    </VerticalStackLayout>
  </DataTemplate>
</CollectionView.ItemTemplate>
</CollectionView>
```

Key Benefits

- Smoother scrolling and better handling of large datasets.

- More flexibility; you can easily use horizontal lists, grids, or grouped layouts.

- Easy customization and styling with native controls.

2. Replace `TableView` and cells with layouts and `CollectionView`.

   `TableView` was a way to display form-style screens or settings pages with different types of cells. In .NET MAUI, you can typically re-create these UIs using layouts (like `VerticalStackLayout`) with controls such as `Label`, `Entry`, `Switch`, and `Button`, or use a grouped `CollectionView` if you need dynamic sections.

   Before (`TableView`):

```
<TableView>
  <TableRoot>
    <TableSection Title="Settings">
      <TextCell Text="Option 1" />
      <SwitchCell Text="Enable Feature" On="True"/>
    </TableSection>
  </TableRoot>
</TableView>
```

After (stacked layout):

```xml
<VerticalStackLayout Padding="12">
  <Label Text="Settings" FontAttributes="Bold" FontSize="20"/>
  <HorizontalStackLayout>
    <Label Text="Option 1" />
  </HorizontalStackLayout>
  <HorizontalStackLayout VerticalOptions="Center">
    <Label Text="Enable Feature" VerticalOptions="Center"/>
    <Switch IsToggled="True" />
  </HorizontalStackLayout>
</VerticalStackLayout>
```

3. Address the "cell" types.

    If your app uses `TextCell`, `ImageCell`, or `SwitchCell` within
    `ListView` or `TableView`, you now define what each item looks like
    using XAML layouts within `CollectionView`'s `DataTemplate`. This
    gives you much more control over your UI, as you can mix controls
    and style them as you like.

    Practical Migration Tips

    - Start by identifying every usage of `ListView`, `TableView`, and cell
      controls in your XAML files.

    - Replace `ListView` with `CollectionView` and map each
      `DataTemplate` accordingly.

    - Refactor `TableView` pages into layouts and standard controls or
      use `CollectionView` with grouping for dynamic lists.

    - Test each change on all platforms, as layouts and interactions can
      differ slightly across devices.

    - Remove any references to deprecated cell types and define item
      layouts using native XAML controls for greater flexibility.

Animation API Modernization

Animations bring your app to life, making transitions feel smooth and interactive. In .NET MAUI on .NET 10, the animation API has been modernized to better fit how developers build responsive, asynchronous applications. The updates are easy to embrace and help you avoid many of the common pitfalls that came with the older approach.

The Move to Async Animation Methods

Previously, animations in Xamarin.Forms and early MAUI versions were triggered using methods like `FadeTo`, `TranslateTo`, or `ScaleTo`, which could result in complicated code when chaining or coordinating multiple animations. These methods often used callbacks or relied on manual task management, making it hard to maintain and debug more advanced animations.

With .NET 10, all core animation methods have moved to asynchronous equivalents, such as `FadeToAsync`, `TranslateToAsync`, and `ScaleToAsync`. These methods leverage the async/await pattern, so you can:

- Await animations directly, keeping your UI logic simple and linear.

- Chain or parallelize animations without callbacks or event handlers.

- Handle cancellation and error conditions better if needed.

Example: Fading a label out, then translating and fading back in

```
await myLabel.FadeToAsync(0, 300);
await myLabel.TranslateToAsync(0, 40, 250);
await myLabel.FadeToAsync(1, 300);
```

This flow is easy to read, and every next animation happens only after the previous one completes.

Practical Usage and Migration Tips

Migrating to the new async animation APIs is straightforward, but here are some tips to make the transition even simpler:

- **Replace sync methods:** Swap calls like FadeTo for FadeToAsync and update the signature of your event handlers to async if you plan to use await.

- **Chain parallel animations:** Use await for sequential animations and Task.WhenAll to run multiple animations at once:

```
await Task.WhenAll(
  view1.FadeToAsync(1),
  view2.FadeToAsync(1)
);
```

- **Handle cancellations for better UX:** The async API lets you pass a CancellationToken, which helps if the user navigates away or if you want to interrupt long-running animations cleanly.

- **Refactor callbacks:** Remove nested lambdas or completion handlers; async/await syntax makes code more readable and maintainable.

- **Testing and backward compatibility:** If you maintain apps targeting previous .NET versions, keep old animation logic isolated so you can switch to *Async methods exclusively in .NET 10 projects.

This update means working with animations is safer and clearer, and your apps will be more responsive to user interactions. Async animation methods fit perfectly into the .NET ecosystem, making it easier for even newer developers to build delightful, polished user experiences.

Platform-Specific Features and Updates

As .NET MAUI grows, it continuously finds ways to fit more naturally on every target platform. Although MAUI aims to make most features work the same across devices, some improvements are designed specifically for certain operating systems to deliver a truly native experience. This section focuses on key updates and changes for iOS and Mac Catalyst in .NET 10, spotlighting both new capabilities and changes that developers need to embrace for compatibility and accessibility.

iOS and Mac Catalyst

On Apple platforms, apps are expected to feel "at home," matching user expectations for design, navigation, and assistive technology. Recent updates to .NET MAUI improve how modal pages are presented and update accessibility patterns to align more closely with the latest Apple frameworks. These adjustments let your apps feel more intuitive and integrated on iPhones, iPads, and Mac desktops.

Modal Pages as Popovers on iOS and Mac Catalyst

With .NET MAUI on .NET 10, modal page presentation on Apple platforms gets a notable upgrade. Instead of always presenting modal pages as full-screen overlays, MAUI now supports displaying them as popovers on iPads and Mac Catalyst by default, mirroring native design conventions. This means when your app needs to show a transient selection, message, or custom view on a larger display, the modal floats elegantly over your current page instead of occupying the entire screen.

This behavior aligns with common iOS and Mac patterns. Popovers are context-aware; based on device and available screen space, MAUI chooses the best way to present content for clarity and ease of use. You don't need to do much in your code: simply calling methods like `Navigation.PushModalAsync(new MyModalPage())` automatically adapts the presentation style. This transition results in less disruptive UI transitions and keeps users oriented within your app, especially on devices supporting multitasking and split views.

If you want to force a full-screen presentation or tweak the style further, you can leverage platform-specific APIs or custom renderers, but for most apps, the default popover experience is the right fit. This change addresses a long-standing request from the developer community and helps new MAUI apps feel consistent with modern Apple guidelines.

Accessibility Extension Deprecations and New Approaches

Accessibility is critical for any modern app, and .NET MAUI strives to make building accessible UIs straightforward. In .NET 10, some older accessibility extension methods and properties, especially those carried forward from Xamarin.Forms, have been deprecated to better align with evolving Apple and platform standards. You might notice warnings for properties or extension methods such as `IsInAccessibleTree` or certain automation event APIs.

Instead, MAUI encourages you to use updated properties and approaches that tap into the native accessibility systems on iOS and macOS:

- **Use properties like `SemanticProperties.Description`, `SemanticProperties.Hint`, and `SemanticProperties.HeadingLevel` to describe interface elements:** These elements attach accessibility information that is platform-agnostic but maps cleanly to `VoiceOver` and other screen readers.

- **For interactive controls, ensure that buttons, images, and custom layouts have descriptive text and use the correct semantic role:** This makes navigation by assistive technologies more natural and reliable.

- **Where possible, group related UI elements together using container semantics:** This helps tools like VoiceOver provide context and skip unnecessary content.

For example, to make a button accessible, use this:

```
<Button Text="Submit"
        SemanticProperties.Description="Saves your changes"
        SemanticProperties.Hint="Double tap to send the form"/>
```

iOS and Mac Catalyst will pick up these semantics, announcing the button's purpose and action clearly to users relying on accessibility tools. Adopting these new properties not only improves compliance but also ensures a broader, more inclusive audience can confidently use your app.

By refactoring your code to use the latest semantic APIs and removing deprecated extensions, you future-proof your apps and doors stay open for more advanced accessibility features down the line.

Android

Android development in .NET MAUI on .NET 10 reaches new heights with better platform support, richer user experiences, and simpler app maintenance. Here's what's new and important for your projects.

Support for Android API 36 and JDK 21

.NET MAUI in .NET 10 now supports targeting the latest Android 16 (API level 36), allowing your apps to take advantage of all recent security, performance, and feature updates from Android. This means you can confidently submit your apps to the Google Play Store, where newer API levels soon become mandatory, while knowing your app works seamlessly with recent devices.

The standard project templates now use Android API 36 by default. You can update your projects to use this by setting the `net10.0-android36` target framework. While projects targeting older APIs (down to API 21) are still supported, updating to API 24 or higher is highly recommended for stability and to prevent runtime issues, especially if you use modern Java language features.

Another major step forward is the adoption of JDK 21 as a supported Java Development Kit. You can now use JDK 21 for building .NET for Android projects, keeping your toolchain aligned with the latest industry standards and tapping into improved build performance and compatibility with modern libraries and Android tooling.

What it means for you:

- **Stay up-to-date:** This future-proofs your apps with the platform's latest features and requirements.

- **Better build performance:** Ongoing under-the-hood changes reduce build times and improve reliability, making development less frustrating.

- **Simple migration:** To use these updates, install Android API 36 with the Android SDK tools, ensure JDK 21 is on your system, and update your project targets.

WebView Fullscreen Video Playback

A common request for Android apps embedding web content is smooth, native-like, full-screen video playback inside WebViews. With .NET MAUI on .NET 10, this is now supported out of the box.

When you load an `<iframe>` with the `allowfullscreen` attribute inside a WebView, users can play videos in true full-screen mode. This brings your app much closer to native Android browsing or video applications, giving users the immersive experience they expect from modern multimedia apps.

To enable full-screen video, make sure your video iframe includes `allowfullscreen`. Here's an example snippet of a WebView displaying a YouTube video:

```
myWebView.Source = new HtmlWebViewSource
{
    Html = @"<!DOCTYPE html>
<html>
<body>
    <iframe width='560' height='315' src='https://www.youtube.com/
    embed/YE7VzlLtp-4' allowfullscreen></iframe>
</body>
</html>"
};
```

No additional custom handlers are needed; this works natively on Android with .NET MAUI 10.

Editor and Entry Native View Changes

Text input is a foundation of almost every app, and this release brings notable improvements to the Editor and Entry controls on Android.

In .NET MAUI 10, these controls have switched from wrapping `AppCompatEditText` to using a custom, modernized `MauiAppCompatEditText`. This update enables several key benefits:

- **SelectionChanged event:** Developers now have access to a native SelectionChanged event, allowing for more responsive UX features like custom toolbars, context menus, and live formatting as users select text.

- **Better integration with native features:** More reliable text input, cursor movement, automatic keyboard behavior, and improved compatibility with accessibility tools.

- **Consistent behavior:** Entry and Editor controls now act more like their pure-Android counterparts, reducing confusing differences between platforms and improving overall app quality.

Quick Example

```
<Entry Placeholder="Your Name" />
<Editor Placeholder="Write your message here..." AutoSize="TextChanges"/>
```

With these improvements, entering, selecting, and editing text in your apps becomes more user-friendly and bug-resistant.

Cross-Platform Improvements

With each release, .NET MAUI gets better at making sure your code works smoothly across all platforms. In .NET 10, developers see meaningful upgrades that make core device features like geolocation and authentication more reliable, predictable, and user-friendly on every device, whether that's Android, iOS, Windows, or Mac.

Geolocation: The New *IsEnabled* Property

The Geolocation API in .NET MAUI traditionally let apps fetch a user's current location with a simple call, but it often left uncertainty about whether location services were available or ready on the device at that moment, which led to avoidable exceptions or confusing fallbacks for users in earlier versions. With .NET 10, the API introduces a new Geolocation.IsEnabled property that provides a straightforward, cross-platform way to check whether location services are enabled before making any request, allowing developers to short-circuit gracefully when the device is not able to provide coordinates. This small addition improves reliability, prevents unnecessary prompts, and creates a smoother experience, especially for beginners building location-aware apps, because feature availability is verified up front.

A minimal pattern now looks like this: check IsEnabled; if it's true, request a location; otherwise, inform the user or direct them to settings.

```
if (Geolocation.Default.IsEnabled)
{
    var location = await Geolocation.Default.GetLocationAsync();
    // Use the location as needed
}
else
```

```
{
    // Inform the user or prompt for permissions/settings
}
```

This property behaves consistently across supported platforms, giving a simple capability check that avoids exceptions when services are off and helps keep the UI responsive.

A Complete Flow with Permissions and Settings

This is a real-world example that ties the new IsEnabled check together with permission handling, a sensible timeout, and a graceful fallback to device settings. It mirrors a very common scenario: centering a map on the user's current position if possible, or guiding the user when it isn't.

```csharp
using Microsoft.Maui.ApplicationModel;
using Microsoft.Maui.Devices.Sensors;
using System.Threading;

public async Task<bool> TryCenterOnUserAsync(CancellationToken ct =
default)
{
    if (!Geolocation.Default.IsEnabled)
    {
        await Shell.Current.DisplayAlert(
            "Location disabled",
            "Turn on Location Services to show your position on the map.",
            "Open Settings",
            "Cancel");
        AppInfo.Current.ShowSettingsUI();

        return false;
    }

    var status = await Permissions.CheckStatusAsync<Permissions.
LocationWhenInUse>();
    if (status != PermissionStatus.Granted)
    {
        status = await Permissions.RequestAsync<Permissions.
LocationWhenInUse>();
```

```
    if (status != PermissionStatus.Granted)
        return false;
}

var request = new GeolocationRequest(GeolocationAccuracy.Medium,
TimeSpan.FromSeconds(10));
try
{
    var location = await Geolocation.Default.
    GetLocationAsync(request, ct);
    if (location is null)
        return false;

     map.Center = new MapSpan(new Location(location.Latitude, location.
     Longitude), 0.01, 0.01);
    map.Pins.Clear();
    map.Pins.Add(new Pin { Location = new Location(location.Latitude,
    location.Longitude), Label = "You are here" });
    return true;
}
catch (FeatureNotEnabledException)
{
    return false;
}
catch (PermissionException)
{
    return false;
}
}
```

This pattern uses `IsEnabled` to avoid dead ends, requests permissions only when necessary using the documented Permissions API, and wraps the location request in a reasonable timeout to protect UX and battery, before finally updating a map, a scenario covered in many practical samples and guides.

Why this approach helps in production apps is simple: it prevents exceptions by verifying capability first, it respects user intent by prompting only when needed, and it provides a clear fallback path to settings when location is disabled, which together reduce friction and support a predictable experience across Android, iOS, Windows, and Mac.

WebAuthenticator: Built-In Support for Cancellation

Many modern apps need to let users log in or authorize actions through the browser; think OAuth for social logins or third-party services. .NET MAUI uses the WebAuthenticator API for this. One challenge common to all platforms, though, is handling the case where a user starts to log in but then cancels or closes the browser.

.NET 10 addresses this by building in cancellation support for the WebAuthenticator component. Now, you can pass a CancellationToken when starting the authentication flow. If the user walks away, presses back, or closes the app, the operation can be cancelled gracefully. No more hanging tasks or confusing error messages.

```
using (var cts = new CancellationTokenSource())
{
    try
    {
        var result = await WebAuthenticator.Default.AuthenticateAsync(
            new Uri("https://example.com/auth"),
            new Uri("myapp://callback"),
            cts.Token); // Pass in the cancellation token
        // Handle successful authentication
    }
    catch (OperationCanceledException)
    {
        // Handle the user cancelling (e.g., show a message or
        simply ignore)
    }
}
```

Now, your app responds properly to user intent. Cancelled or abandoned login flows do not lead to frozen screens or broken sessions. This makes authentication more robust and user-friendly and lets you create cross-platform login experiences that feel truly native.

Modernizing Media and File Pickers

.NET MAUI in .NET 10 makes it much simpler and far more powerful to add media and file selection features to your apps. With new capabilities for picking, editing, and validating images or files, as well as smarter controls for handling dates and times, your apps become more user-friendly and flexible. This section covers what's new and why it matters.

MediaPicker Improvements: Resize, Compress, and EXIF Support

The MediaPicker API lets apps capture or choose photos and videos directly from a device's gallery or camera, and in .NET 10 it's been modernized to handle common real-world needs without extra libraries or complex code. On mobile, where bandwidth and storage matter, being able to control the size, quality, and metadata up front makes everyday tasks, like uploading profile photos or attaching receipts, faster and more reliable.

On-the-fly image resizing and compression means the app no longer has to accept whatever resolution the camera provides. When a user picks or captures a photo, the app can request specific dimensions and a quality level before the image is returned, keeping upload sizes small and storage usage under control. This protects users on slow connections and helps maintain responsive interfaces during uploads. A minimal pattern looks like this: pick a photo and apply resize and compression options directly in the request.

```
var options = new MediaPickerOptions
{
    Resize = new ResizeOption { Width = 800, Height = 600 },
    CompressionQuality = 80 // 0 (lowest) .. 100 (highest)
};

var result = await MediaPicker.Default.PickPhotoAsync(options);
```

For photos, EXIF metadata—such as when an image was taken, its camera orientation, or the location where it was captured—can now be read as part of the same flow. This enables smarter features like chronological sorting, automatic rotation, or geotag-aware galleries without additional parsing. A basic example reads EXIF after the user picks a photo.

```
if (result != null)
{
    using var stream = await result.OpenReadAsync();
    var exifData = await ExifReader.Default.ReadAsync(stream);
    var takenDate = exifData.DateTimeOriginal;
}
```

The picker is also more flexible when working with documents. Apps can specify accepted file types up front, which prevents users from selecting unsupported formats and reduces server-side validation errors before an upload even starts. This keeps flows like expense submissions or resume uploads simple and consistent across platforms.

A Practical Example

The following example shows how to upload a profile picture with size limits and metadata. It combines the new capabilities into a short, production-friendly flow. The user selects a profile photo. The app ensures the image is right-sized and compressed for upload, preserves EXIF capture time for auditing, and shows a small preview. This is a common pattern in social, commerce, or enterprise apps.

```
var pickOptions = new MediaPickerOptions
{

    Resize = new ResizeOption { Width = 1024, Height = 1024 },
    CompressionQuality = 75
};

var file = await MediaPicker.Default.PickPhotoAsync(pickOptions);
if (file is null)
{
    await Shell.Current.DisplayAlert("No photo", "No image was
selected.", "OK");
    return;
}

DateTimeOffset? takenAt = null;
using (var exifStream = await file.OpenReadAsync())
{
    var exif = await ExifReader.Default.ReadAsync(exifStream);
    takenAt = exif.DateTimeOriginal ?? exif.DateTimeDigitized;
```

```
}

using var uploadStream = await file.OpenReadAsync();
using var content = new MultipartFormDataContent
{
    { new StreamContent(uploadStream), "file", file.FileName },
    { new StringContent(takenAt?.ToString("o") ?? string.Empty),
"takenAt" }
};

using var client = new HttpClient { BaseAddress = new Uri("https://api.
example.com/") };
var response = await client.PostAsync("users/me/profile-photo", content);
if (!response.IsSuccessStatusCode)
{
    await Shell.Current.DisplayAlert("Upload failed", "Please try a
different image.", "OK");
    return;
}

 profileImage.Source = ImageSource.FromStream(() => file.OpenReadAsync().
Result);
await Shell.Current.DisplayToastAsync("Profile photo updated.");
```

Why this helps in real apps is straightforward: The image is already resized and compressed when it reaches the app, so uploads are faster and more predictable across different devices and camera hardware; EXIF capture time can be stored for later use (for example, to sort a gallery or verify when a picture was taken); and by constraining file types in pickers for documents, common mistakes are prevented early in the flow. Together, these improvements reduce server load, make UIs more responsive, and remove edge cases that used to require extra code or third-party libraries.

Nullable *DatePicker* and *TimePicker* Controls

Handling dates and times in forms used to be tricky, especially when selecting a value was optional. Previously, `DatePicker` and `TimePicker` in .NET MAUI always required a value, and there was no straightforward way to clear the selection or represent a "not set" state.

With .NET 10, both controls are now nullable, meaning your users can skip the selection, or you can easily clear a previously set value from your code.

- **Clearable selection:** Users can now tap a clear or reset action to remove a date or time value instead of picking a default or dummy value.

- **Data binding improvements:** Bound objects can treat nulls as truly "not selected," leading to cleaner, more accurate form submission logic.

```
<DatePicker x:Name="datePicker" Date="{Binding SelectedDate,
Mode=TwoWay}" />
<Button Text="Clear Date" Command="{Binding ClearDateCommand}" />
```

And in your view model or code-behind:

```
SelectedDate = null; // This clears the date picker.
```

The same pattern now works with `TimePicker`, enabling better user experiences for forms, scheduling, or any case where a date or time input should be optional.

Performance and Quality Improvements

Every new release of .NET MAUI focuses on making apps not just easier to build, but faster and more reliable for your users. With .NET 10, the platform delivers a noticeable boost in performance and quality, resulting in apps that feel quicker, use less memory, and are more stable overall.

Overview of Performance Boosts and Bug Fixes

In .NET 10, significant work has gone into optimizing the internal code paths of MAUI, reducing the time it takes for key operations like loading the first page, rendering complex layouts, or switching between screens. Areas that once slowed down large or graphics-heavy apps such as resource management and control rendering have been streamlined. Many memory leaks found in previous versions have been eliminated, leading to fewer unexpected crashes and lower memory use on mobile devices.

There have also been hundreds of targeted bug fixes throughout the MAUI framework. These range from eliminating glitches in layout measurement and control sizing to smoothing out focus and input issues for text fields and interactive controls. Developers report improved reliability in data binding, navigation, and visual updates thanks to these behind-the-scenes changes.

Impact on App Startup, Rendering, and Memory Usage

- **Faster app startup:** Many MAUI apps now launch more quickly on both cold and warm starts. .NET 10 has introduced improvements like reduced assembly loading times, better dependency resolution, and more aggressive resource preloading. On average, users will see splash screens disappear sooner and first screens render with noticeably less delay.

- **Smoother rendering:** Rendering, how your UI appears and updates, has become more efficient across all supported platforms. Animation performance is more consistent, and complex layouts update without lag or stutter, thanks to optimized rendering pipelines and new default control handlers. As a result, user interactions feel snappier, especially on older or mid-range devices.

- **Lower memory usage:** Apps spend less time using high amounts of RAM, even as screen complexity grows. Memory management improvements mean that unused resources are released more intelligently, and backend processes are less likely to grow out of control as users navigate back and forth within the app. This is especially helpful on devices with limited memory or when running apps alongside other heavy workloads.

- **Longer running stability:** All these enhancements combine to reduce the likelihood of "resource starvation" and random crashes, both common in previous versions when background tasks or heavy UI updates were involved. As a result, users are less likely to report slowdowns, freezes, or force-closes as their usage grows.

Together, the performance upgrades and quality fixes in .NET MAUI for .NET 10 mean your apps will start faster, run smoother, and behave more predictably, giving both new and experienced developers greater confidence as they build for any platform.

Summary and Next Steps

Reaching the end of this journey through what's new in .NET MAUI for .NET 10, you can truly see how the platform has matured. The latest release is all about making your app-building process easier, the results more polished, and learning MAUI more approachable than ever.

Recap of the Most Important Changes

.NET MAUI in .NET 10 introduces a collection of focused updates that simplify development and greatly enhance app performance. One of the most noticeable shifts is the move away from older controls like `ListView` and `TableView`, replaced by the faster and more flexible `CollectionView` and `CarouselView`. These new controls handle larger datasets, enable complex layouts, and feel snappier in every interaction.

Other controls have gained new capabilities as well, including cleaner customization for things like the `SearchBar` and `Switch`, and expanded community support for controls such as `ColorPicker` and `DockLayout`. This means you can build more professional interfaces with less custom code. Under the hood, core features like the animation API have been modernized to use `async` patterns, making it easier to deliver smooth, coordinated visual experiences.

Major improvements have also landed in platform-specific support. Developers can now target the latest Android API levels and JDK 21, ensure popovers and accessibility on iOS and Mac fit modern guidelines, and use features like nullable pickers and advanced media handling consistently on all devices. Together with a suite of small but impactful quality and performance updates, MAUI apps now start faster, run with less memory, and crash less often.

Recommendations for Developers New to MAUI or .NET 10

For beginners, the path into .NET MAUI has never been more straightforward. Starting a new project with the updated templates ensures you benefit from the default choices like `CollectionView` for lists and `async` animations for best results out of the box. As you learn, focus on understanding how to use the new async API patterns and take advantage of built-in features for theming, accessibility, and platform targeting without reaching for custom solutions too quickly.

If you're moving from earlier versions or from Xamarin.Forms, approach migration gradually: swap out deprecated controls, apply global namespaces in XAML, and adopt the new `MediaPicker` and authentication features to modernize your codebase. Rely on MAUI's strong data binding and native control handlers for smoother, more reliable interfaces. Always test on each platform you plan to support to ensure a consistent user experience and uncover subtle differences early, rather than late in your development process.

Try to build your projects in small pieces, testing early and often. This will help you understand both the power and the cross-platform consistency of MAUI.

CHAPTER 7

Performance and Optimization

Introduction

These days, one of the most crucial aspects of developing any app is performance. Consumers anticipate that everything will be quick and easy. Users don't tolerate slow software, regardless of whether it is a large web service or a mobile app. Speed is not the only factor in good performance. Additionally, your app needs to run smoothly on a variety of devices and use less memory. Your code is much better for everyone when it runs more quickly and consumes fewer resources.

Why Performance Matters in Modern Apps

Everyone uses apps on various devices in today's world. Every day, people use phones, tablets, laptops, and even outdated computers. People will close or uninstall your app if it is sluggish or uses excessive amounts of memory. If you have to run slow apps on servers, it can also cost more money, particularly if your app becomes popular and many users use it simultaneously.

Efficiency is important to businesses as well. A quick app can use less hardware and support more users. This translates into cost savings and satisfaction for all parties involved, including users and server owners.

Key Themes in .NET 10: Reducing Abstraction, Lowering Memory Usage, and Generating Smarter Code

Numerous features in .NET 10 are designed to improve the speed and fluidity of your code. Reducing abstraction is one crucial concept. Code may run more slowly if it is overly abstract or has too many layers. The goal of .NET 10 is to simplify common code paths and bring them closer to what your processor can rapidly execute.

Another important thing is to use less memory. Your app will function better on devices with limited resources if it uses less memory. It also means your app can run longer without any problems and you can avoid slowdowns caused by things like garbage collection.

The key to smarter code generation is transforming your C# code into something the computer can run as efficiently as possible by .NET 10. This entails speeding up loops, enhancing array functionality, and allowing the system to determine what can be optimized while your application is running.

What to Expect in this Chapter

In this chapter, you discover:

- Why performance is a core goal in .NET 10

- The main improvements in how .NET 10 runs your code more quickly

- Real examples that show exactly what's changed and how you can use these features

- Simple, hands-on code examples to help you see the difference

You don't have to be an expert to follow along. Every section explains the main ideas in simple words. I want you to feel comfortable as you learn new techniques. By the end, you'll know what's new in .NET 10 and understand how to make your own apps run even better.

The .NET 10 Optimization Philosophy

Focusing on Real-World Developer Scenarios

The enhancements in .NET 10 go beyond merely impressing benchmark figures. Solving issues that regular developers encounter has always been the aim. The .NET team carefully considered the feedback from developers of actual applications, whether they be desktop programs, mobile tools, or heavily trafficked web APIs.

Teams that wanted their apps to run better on small devices and large cloud servers, use less memory, and start up faster initiated many of the changes in .NET 10. The platform now addresses issues with large data processing and UI-heavy apps by concentrating on areas where minor code modifications result in significant performance improvements for daily use.

Balancing Runtime Speed, Memory Efficiency, and Code Simplicity

In addition to speeding up code execution, .NET 10 optimizations are made to keep things easy for developers. The team put a lot of effort into coming up with solutions that boost performance without requiring you to write intricate, difficult-to-read code.

You will see enhancements to the JIT compiler that make code more efficient in the background, as well as features that optimize common patterns, like working with collections or iterating through arrays. Memory usage is also given a lot of attention. Your apps can grow and accommodate more users without requiring additional work from the developers, thanks to improved memory management, more intelligent garbage collection, and more effective resource allocation.

You do not have to choose between readable and fast code because of this balance. Most of the time, simply updating to the latest version of .NET 10 makes a big difference due to its smarter engine.

Continuous Journey from .NET Core to Latest Release

.NET's journey from its early days through .NET Core and now to .NET 10 has been shaped by constant improvement. Each release, starting with .NET Core, has aimed to make things better for both developers and users. With every version, the team has worked to fix the pain points discovered in real apps.

For example, previous versions of .NET made big strides in cross-platform performance and in supporting cloud workloads. Each release since then—.NET Core 3, .NET 5, 6, 7, 8, and 9—added new layers of optimization, such as tiered compilation, smaller SDK footprints, and cutting down on memory needed to run web services. .NET 10 builds on all this, delivering tools and enhancements shaped by years of lessons from real applications and the people who build them.

By focusing on real-life coding situations and practical feedback, .NET 10 makes it easier for developers to write efficient, clear, and modern apps, without starting from scratch or learning complicated tricks.

JIT Compiler Enhancements

Improved Layout of Method Code Blocks for Better CPU Caching and Pipelining

.NET 10 introduces significant improvements in how the JIT compiler organizes your method's code. The JIT now uses a new strategy to place parts of your method that are frequently executed, often called *hot paths,* close together in memory. This helps your processor keep those instructions ready in its cache, which allows your code to run faster and reduces the time lost to unnecessary branching and memory delays.

By laying out code blocks with the "hot" (frequently run) code grouped tightly, .NET 10 makes better use of the CPU instruction cache and improves the efficiency of instruction pipelining. The result is smoother execution, especially in methods with complex control flow or tight loops. Unlike before, where only certain block orderings were considered, the new approach uses a mathematical model like solving a travel route so that the "hot" blocks are traversed with fewer jumps and cache misses.

Loop Inversion and Optimizations for Common Loops

Loop inversion is a common optimization where the JIT transforms a `while` loop into a `do-while` loop. This change reduces the number of jumps required to check the loop condition, letting the CPU process the loop body more efficiently. .NET 10 improves how it detects and inverts loops, using a more intelligent, graph-based algorithm. This allows .NET to better recognize all natural loops (loops with a single entry), ignore non-loops, and open other advanced loop optimizations (like loop unrolling or variable hoisting).

Example Before (a Classic `while` Loop)

```
int i = 0;
while (i < n)
{
    Process(i);
    i++;
}
```

After Inversion (JIT Does This Internally)

```
int i = 0;
if (i < n)
{
    do
    {
        Process(i);
        i++;
    } while (i < n);
}
```

This technique helps reduce jump instructions in the final machine code, making iterations slightly faster, especially in performance-critical code paths.

Example Scenarios: Array Loops and Struct Method Calls

These smarter optimizations are not just theory; they have a tangible impact on real-world code. For example:

- **Array loops:** .NET 10 can now detect the pattern when you loop through an array and optimize it, even when you use interfaces like `IEnumerable`. The JIT can eliminate virtual calls and unnecessary object allocations, making such code nearly as fast as using a direct for loop over the array. For instance, iterating over arrays using a foreach with an `IEnumerable` allocation used to be slow, but now, the allocation and virtual call overhead are gone.

Before (with Overhead)

```
int[] numbers = { 1, 2, 3, 4, 5 };
IEnumerable enumerable = numbers;
foreach (int num in enumerable)
```

```
{
    Console.Write(num + " ");
}
```

After Optimization (No Overhead)

```
int[] numbers = { 1, 2, 3, 4, 5 };
foreach (int num in numbers)
{
    Console.Write(num + " ");
}
```

In .NET 10, both examples have similar performance, and the unnecessary allocation is removed.

- **Struct method calls:** The JIT now promotes struct data so that when you pass a struct to a method, its members can live in processor registers, making access faster and reducing memory access.

A struct Example

```
struct Point
{
    public int X;
    public int Y;
}
void HandlePoint(Point p)
{
    Console.WriteLine(p.X + p.Y);
}
```

.NET 10's smarter code generation puts X and Y together into the processor registers, so there are fewer memory references when calling HandlePoint.

Overall, these improvements mean your existing code gets faster automatically after upgrading to .NET 10. You gain better loop performance, smarter memory use, and lower CPU usage without changing your code style.

Devirtualization and Inlining Improvements
Array Interface Method Devirtualization

.NET 10 includes important changes to how array methods are optimized when accessed through interfaces. In older versions, looping over an array via an interface like IEnumerable<T> caused the JIT compiler to generate extra layers of calls, adding a performance overhead. These virtual calls prevented certain optimizations such as inlining, stack allocation, and loop unrolling.

Starting with .NET 10, the JIT can now recognize and optimize array interface methods. For example, iterating over an array directly or casting it as IEnumerable<int> used to have notable performance differences. Now, the JIT often devirtualizes calls, reducing unnecessary object creation and virtual dispatch, so a foreach loop over IEnumerable<int> is closer in speed to looping directly over the array.

Code Example Before .NET 10 (Higher Overhead)

```
int[] numbers = { 1, 2, 3, 4, 5 };
IEnumerable<int> enumerable = numbers;
foreach (int num in enumerable) // Virtual call to GetEnumerator()
{
    Console.Write(num + " ");
}
```

Code Example After .NET 10 (Optimized)

```
int[] numbers = { 1, 2, 3, 4, 5 };
foreach (int num in numbers) // JIT eliminates the virtual call!
{
    Console.Write(num + " ");
}
```

The difference is significant in larger datasets or inside hot code paths, with the interface overhead reduced to almost negligible levels in many scenarios.

Inlining of Late Devirtualized Methods

Only when the JIT identified early that a virtual call could be substituted with a direct call (devirtualizing) could it inline methods in earlier .NET versions. The JIT could only determine that it was safe to devirtualize specific virtual calls after inlining, which occasionally reveals more details about concrete types. The JIT more efficiently monitors these opportunities in .NET 10. The JIT can now inline that call as well if a method qualifies for devirtualization during or after inlining, increasing the depth of optimization and causing tight performance loops to improve.

Practical Impact

Because the JIT can fold methods in and eliminate superfluous layers, methods that use delegates or interface-based patterns become more effective.

Devirtualization Based on Inlining Observations

With .NET 10, the JIT further devirtualizes method calls by using information it finds during inlining. The JIT examines what each return site returns when the result of an inlined call is stored in a temporary variable. The JIT modifies the variable's type information if each return type is the same precise concrete type. This simplifies LINQ method chains and blocks by enabling the devirtualization of the subsequent method call.

A factory method that returns an interface but each branch returns the same type is an example scenario. Even if the subsequent calls take place through the interface, the JIT will use this information to optimize them.

Impact on Abstraction Penalty and Real-World LINQ or *IEnumerable* Scenarios

These compiler advancements directly reduce the *abstraction penalty,* which is the cost incurred when using general-purpose interfaces or LINQ in your code. Historically, using IEnumerable<T>, IReadOnlyList<T>, or LINQ queries came with a performance tradeoff compared to specialized loops because of virtual calls and heap allocations. In .NET 10, these penalties are much lower:

- **Benchmarks show:** In .NET 9, iterating an array as `IEnumerable<T>` could incur an 80% or greater performance cost over direct array use. In .NET 10, this drops to about 10% or less, with allocations eliminated in many hot path situations.

- **LINQ improvements:** LINQ methods like `select`, `where`, `sum`, and so on—when operating over arrays or commonly returned types—benefit from inlining, devirtualization, and smart memory management. While LINQ itself still involves delegates and enumerators, the JIT removes much of the virtual dispatch, letting code run almost as fast as handwritten loops.

Escape Analysis and Stack Allocation

Escape Analysis for Better Lifetime Management

In .NET 10, the JIT compiler uses escape analysis to determine if an object or array created inside a method ever "escapes" the method's scope. If the object is never used outside the method, the JIT knows its lifetime is very short and predictable. This means the compiler can keep that object on the stack, rather than allocating space for it on the heap.

Previously, almost all objects and arrays were created on the heap, even if they were only used briefly inside a single method. This caused extra work for the garbage collector and could slow down your app, especially in performance-critical code or hot loops. Now, with escape analysis, .NET 10 can be smarter about object lifetimes, producing faster and more memory-efficient code.

Stack Allocation for Small Arrays of Value Types and Reference Types

One of the most useful optimizations from escape analysis is stack allocation, especially for small arrays and structs. When the JIT detects that an array (either of value types like `int` or reference types like `string`) doesn't leave the method, it can allocate that array directly on the stack. Stack allocation is much cheaper than heap allocation and automatically cleans up memory when the stack frame goes away at the end of the method.

Previously, stack allocation was limited mostly to structs and small Span<T>/ stackalloc cases. Now, .NET 10 extends this benefit to arrays and a wider range of use cases, so short-lived collections can be safer and faster.

Example: Stack Allocation of a Small Value-Type Array

```
void ProcessItems()
{
    int[] localArray = new int[8]; // The JIT allocates this array on the
                                      stack if it never escapes
    for (int i = 0; i < localArray.Length; i++)
        localArray[i] = i * i;
    // localArray is cleaned up automatically on method exit
}
```

The same idea can apply to arrays of references when their use does not escape the method.

Practical Benefits: Reduced Garbage Collection and Faster Loop Operations

These optimizations deliver several real-world benefits:

- **Less garbage collection:** Objects and arrays on the stack don't add to GC pressure, so apps experience fewer GC pauses and can handle more users or requests at once.

- **Faster loop operations:** When arrays live on the stack, you avoid heap allocation cost, memory fragmentation, and GC overhead. This makes tight loops run faster, which is especially helpful in math-heavy routines, serialization code, or scenarios where many small objects are rapidly created and destroyed.

- **Predictable memory use:** Stack storage is managed automatically, ensuring memory is always freed at the end of method execution and reducing the chance of memory leaks.

These improvements happen behind the scenes. As a developer, you don't need to write any special code; just write regular C# and let .NET 10 do the work of optimizing your variables and arrays for you. This way, your apps are easier to read and naturally faster, thanks to the latest advances in .NET's runtime and compiler engines.

Array Enumeration Deabstraction

Direct Array Iteration vs. *IEnumerable* Penalties

Direct `foreach` loops were always far faster than `IEnumerable` or comparable interfaces when it came to iterating over arrays in earlier.NET versions. This discrepancy, referred to as the *abstraction penalty,* resulted from the introduction of virtual method calls and occasionally needless heap allocations by `IEnumerable`. The JIT compiler was unable to effectively optimize the loop when the precise type of collection was concealed from it.

This disparity is evident from benchmarks from previous iterations: in .NET 9, iterating over an array with `IEnumerable` could be more than five times slower than using a plain array loop, and additional allocations would also be required.

Reduction of Cost When Using Abstraction in Code

.NET 10 delivers a major improvement by almost erasing this abstraction penalty. The runtime applies new JIT optimizations such as array interface method devirtualization, inlining, enhanced escape analysis, and stack allocation for certain enumerators. These enhancements let the JIT recognize when an array hides behind an interface and optimize the code as if it were iterating the array directly.

- Virtual calls in common patterns like `foreach` are either turned into direct calls or eliminated, so more code can be inlined and optimized.

- Stack allocation removes unnecessary heap allocations for the enumerator in many methods.

- Loop invariants and control flows are recognized intelligently, so common enumerator logic can become almost as efficient as a tight `for` or `foreach` loop.

These changes mean that using abstractions like `IEnumerable` and `IReadOnlyList` with arrays are no longer automatic performance traps.

Concrete Benchmarks and Real Impact

Recent benchmarks clearly show the reduction in overhead between the two approaches in .NET 10 compared to .NET 9, as shown in the following table.

Loop Method	.NET 9	.NET 10	Relative Overhead (vs. Direct)	Allocation
foreach on direct array	150 ns	150 ns	1.00x	None
foreach on array via interface	851 ns	280 ns	5.65x -> 1.86x	None

In practice, that means the extra cost of writing code like this is now almost gone:

```
IEnumerable<int> data = array;
foreach (int value in data)
{
    // work
}
```

Where .NET 9 would have made this code run noticeably slower (sometimes with more than 80% overhead), .NET 10 reduces it to less than 10% overhead in typical real-world apps.

These improvements are especially impactful for codebases that rely on abstraction, reusable libraries, or the LINQ pipeline. Developers can now write cleaner, more maintainable code using interfaces, with confidence that performance remains solid.

Stack Allocation of Arrays

When and How Value-Type and Reference-Type Arrays Are Stack-Allocated

In .NET 10, stack allocation of arrays has become much more powerful and general. The runtime, thanks to smarter escape analysis, can allocate small arrays of both value types (like int and double) and reference types (like string) on the stack when it determines that the lifetime of those arrays doesn't go beyond the containing method.

Value-Type Arrays

Before .NET 10, stack allocation was mostly limited to certain stack-based constructs like Span<T> and specific cases with `stackalloc`. Now, the JIT can decide, for small, fixed-sized arrays of value types that don't include references, whether to place the array on the stack automatically. This happens if the array:

- Is not captured by a delegate or returned from the method.

- Doesn't escape the local scope in any way.

Example

```
static void Sum()
{
    int[] numbers = { 1, 2, 3 };
    int sum = 0;
    for (int i = 0; i < numbers.Length; i++)
        sum += numbers[i];
    Console.WriteLine(sum);
}
```

In this example, the numbers array is only used within sum. The JIT will stack-allocate it, eliminating any heap allocation.

Reference-Type Arrays

.NET 10 takes this feature a big step further. Small arrays of reference types, such as string[], are now candidates for stack allocation as long as their lifetime is scoped to the method. Previous versions always put these on the heap, but .NET 10 can now put arrays like string[] words = { "Hello", "World!" }; on the stack if the JIT can prove that they won't escape.

Example

```
static void Print()
{
    string[] words = { "Hello", "World!" };
    foreach (var str in words)
        Console.WriteLine(str);
}
```

Here, the `words` array gets stack-allocated, making the method faster and more memory-efficient.

How the JIT Decides

The JIT's decision relies on escape analysis: if it can guarantee the array's whole lifetime is inside the method, it puts it on the stack; otherwise, it falls back to the heap. Even arrays assigned to local fields in `structs` can be stack-allocated, provided the `struct` itself does not escape the local method.

GC Pressure Reduction and Application Startup Speed

Stack allocation reduces garbage collection (GC) pressure in two important ways:

- **Lower GC load:** Objects on the stack do not become part of the heap, so the garbage collector has fewer objects to track and fewer pauses to perform. This means fewer and shorter GC pauses overall, making your application feel smoother and more responsive, which is especially important in high-throughput or low-latency scenarios like games, web servers, and real-time applications.

- **Faster startup:** Because fewer allocations happen on the heap during startup, routines that use small, temporary arrays, applications can start up and initialize state faster. This is especially noticeable in scenarios with a lot of transient object creation in the early phases of the app.

Performance Impact

According to benchmarks, scenarios that previously required heap allocations (and consequently garbage collection) now operate up to 60% faster for specific types of short-lived array usage thanks to stack allocation. You do not have to be concerned about manual cleanup or residual memory usage because stack memory is automatically recovered at the conclusion of the method.

Practical Takeaways

- You don't need to change your C# code to enjoy these improvements; just use regular array declarations for temporary arrays with local scope.

- Avoid returning arrays or storing them in fields that outlive the method if you want them to be stack-allocated.

- Take advantage of this by writing clear, method-scoped logic for temporary array usage.

Region-Based GC Information

New APIs for Introspection: *GC.GetMemoryInfo* Improvements

.NET 10 brings enhanced visibility into the runtime's memory management by expanding the capabilities of GC.GetMemoryInfo(). This API now exposes detailed information about the garbage collector's (GC) regions, which are the main organizational units for the heap on 64-bit systems. With the new properties, you can obtain:

- **Region count:** The total number of GC regions currently active.

- **Region size:** The size in bytes of each region (for example, typically 4 MB for the small object heap).

- **Additional region details:** Other metrics relevant to analyzing GC behavior.

This level of transparency helps developers and operators better understand how memory is used in their applications, moving beyond basic metrics like total memory allocated or GC collection counts.

Sample Use

```
var info = GC.GetMemoryInfo();
Console.WriteLine($"GC using {info.RegionCount} regions of
{info.RegionSizeBytes} bytes each");
```

This reveals not just how much memory your app is using but how it is divided, and it can point to inefficiencies tied to memory fragmentation.

Using Region Info to Troubleshoot Memory Fragmentation

Memory fragmentation occurs when small gaps are scattered throughout the heap, making it difficult to allocate large contiguous blocks, even if the total free memory should be sufficient. Understanding region layout and usage is especially important for diagnosing or preventing issues on long-running services or applications that perform many allocations and deallocations over time.

With the updated region-based information, you can:

- **Identify unexpected region growth:** By tracking the RegionCount and RegionSizeBytes, you can see if your app is using more regions than expected, which may signal fragmentation.

- **Correlate GC behavior to application patterns:** If you observe a consistently growing region count or poor compaction results, it may point to large object heap (LOH) fragmentation or unbalanced object lifetimes.

- **Tune GC settings and allocation patterns:** Armed with region insights, you can adjust environment variables like DOTNET_ GCRegionSize (to change region size) or System.GC.RegionRange (to restrict memory use). Reducing region size can help if your app has a small working set and many heaps, while increasing it can be useful in high-load scenarios.

Example: Monitoring Regions for Fragmentation

```
var info = GC.GetMemoryInfo();
if (info.FragmentedBytes > threshold)
{
    Console.WriteLine("High heap fragmentation detected!");
    // Consider triggering a manual GC.Collect() or reviewing allocation
patterns.
}
```

Developers can also use this information when planning workloads with large or variable-sized objects. For applications sensitive to memory fragmentation, such as those that periodically experience allocation failures or `OutOfMemory` exceptions, these insights are essential for both diagnosis and preventive tuning. You may choose to refactor how large objects are allocated, batch allocations, or avoid holding on to objects over 85 KB on the heap for extended periods.

Improved Arm64 Write-Barriers

Details on Better Collection Performance on Arm64 Systems

.NET 10 introduces important improvements to garbage collection performance on Arm64 devices. The platform's garbage collector (GC) is generational, separating memory into regions based on the age of objects. This approach helps collect memory more efficiently by focusing on younger objects that are more likely to become unused quickly.

To manage object references between different generations, .NET uses *write-barriers.* These are small code snippets inserted before reference updates to let the GC track which older objects point to younger ones. Previously, the implementation of write-barriers on Arm64 was less optimized, leading to higher overhead compared to x64 systems and negatively impacting overall application speed.

.NET 10 changes this by introducing a new, more precise default write-barrier for Arm64. Now, Arm64 systems such as Apple M-series and Azure Ampere benefit from a design that keeps the GC informed with less extra work and more accurate region tracking. This minimizes the need to rescan large areas of memory and leads to improved throughput during garbage collection cycles.

Default Write-Barrier Changes and Their Effect on Pause Times

The update to the default write-barrier on Arm64 is a big step forward for application responsiveness. Unlike previous versions where Arm64 could be significantly slower during memory collection phases, the revised barrier design is now more precise and efficient. It reduces the amount of unnecessary memory scans that the GC must perform, especially during high-load scenarios or in long-running services.

Benchmarks on production Arm64 hardware have shown meaningful improvements with these new defaults. GC pause times—the brief periods when your app is paused so that unused objects can be collected—can drop by 8% to over 20% on some workloads compared to earlier versions. This means smoother app experiences and better use of processor resources, especially on devices where efficient battery and hardware usage are critical.

While the new write-barrier may introduce a slight cost to write throughput in some microbenchmarks, the overall benefits from fewer and shorter GC pauses outweigh this small tradeoff. This leads to a net gain in real-world application performance, particularly for web servers, background services, and interactive apps running on modern Arm64 chips.

In summary, these changes allow developers targeting Arm64 to achieve more predictable and efficient memory management with less tuning. Apps built for .NET 10 can expect improved pause times, better responsiveness, and superior scaling because of the updated GC and write-barrier implementation.

Thread Pool Metrics and Monitoring

New APIs to Monitor Thread Pool Health and Behavior

.NET 10 places a strong emphasis on giving developers deeper insight into the behavior and health of the thread pool. Managing the thread pool is critical for apps that rely on concurrency, as it determines how efficiently background tasks and parallel operations are executed.

To make this easier, .NET provides APIs to directly check the health of the thread pool at runtime:

- **`ThreadPool.GetAvailableThreads(out workerThreads, out completionPortThreads)`:** This method returns the number of worker and I/O completion threads that are currently available. It's useful for tracking how many threads are in use versus how many are idle.

- **`ThreadPool.GetMinThreads(out workerThreads, out completionPortThreads)` and `ThreadPool.GetMaxThreads(out ...)`:** These methods let you inspect and tune the pool size limits for worker and I/O threads.

- **Diagnostic and metrics tools:** .NET developers can also use performance counters, event tracing tools (such as `dotnet-counters`), and built-in diagnostic APIs to access real-time thread pool metrics like thread count, queue length, and throughput. Tools like Visual Studio Diagnostic Tools and PerfView can help visualize thread use over time.

You can also configure thread pool parameters based on the unique needs of your app, such as boosting the minimum thread count to respond to traffic spikes or monitoring how the queue backlog responds to bursts of work.

Sample Code for Monitoring Available Threads

```
int worker, io;
ThreadPool.GetAvailableThreads(out worker, out io);
Console.WriteLine($"ThreadPool: {worker} worker, {io} I/O threads
available");
```

Optimizing for High-Throughput, Scalable Applications

For modern cloud services, APIs, and high-traffic apps, optimizing the use of the thread pool is key to performance and scalability:

- **Task reuse and scaling:** The .NET thread pool automatically adapts to workload changes, spinning up new threads under load and scaling back during lulls. This helps reduce the overhead associated with manual thread creation and deletion.

- **Avoiding starvation:** Thread pool starvation occurs when all threads are busy and new requests must wait in a queue. By monitoring metrics like queue length (`ThreadPool.PendingWorkItemCount`) and thread count, you can spot bottlenecks early and adjust your concurrency strategy.

- **`Async/await` patterns:** Leveraging `async` and `await` for I/O-bound operations allows .NET to release thread pool threads while waiting, freeing them to handle other tasks and boosting overall throughput.

- **Tuning `ThreadPool` limits:** For particularly demanding workloads, you can use `ThreadPool.SetMinThreads()` to ensure a higher baseline of ready threads for sudden bursts, reducing cold-start latency. However, raising limits too high can lead to excessive context switching and system contention, so any tuning should be measured and tested under load.

Best Practices

- Regularly profile your application with tools like `dotnet-counters`, PerfView, or Visual Studio Diagnostics.

- Choose non-blocking, async code to avoid tying up thread pool resources.

- Monitor both total thread count and queue length in production for early signs of bottlenecks.

- Tune thread pool settings only as needed. .NET's defaults are well-optimized for most cases, but high-end scenarios may benefit from custom tuning.

By understanding and monitoring thread pool metrics, you can identify performance issues before they impact users, build scalable applications, and get the most out of your hardware and cloud resources. This will give you confidence in building apps that remain responsive and stable, even as demand grows.

Real-World Parallelism Tweaks

Updates to Library Concurrency Primitives

.NET 10 continues to modernize and enhance its collection of concurrency primitives and concurrent data structures. These are foundational building blocks that let developers safely share data and coordinate work across multiple threads in both UI and server-side environments.

Key updates include:

- **Concurrent collections:** Improvements and optimizations for `ConcurrentDictionary<T>`, `ConcurrentBag<T>`, and `ConcurrentQueue<T>`, making them even faster under heavy concurrency by reducing contention and improving scalability for add, remove, and enumerate operations.

- **Synchronization primitives:** The classic `lock` statement continues to be used for simple mutual exclusion. For advanced needs, primitives such as `SemaphoreSlim`, `ReaderWriterLockSlim`, and `ManualResetEventSlim` have received ongoing adjustments for performance and responsiveness.

- **Thread-safe patterns:** The recommendation is now to use high-level thread-safe collections and patterns as much as possible. Using `task`, `async`/`await`, and the parallel loops from the Task Parallel Library (TPL)—like `Parallel.For` and `Parallel.ForEach`—is encouraged for work that can be split into independent chunks.

There are also ongoing developments in community libraries, such as distributed locks for multi-machine scenarios and abstractions that extend the platform's core primitives for specialized use cases.

Practical Guidance for Developers

Here's how you can take advantage of .NET 10's concurrency improvements in your own projects:

- **Choose higher-level concurrency:** Most everyday parallel work can be handled with TPL constructs (`Parallel.For`, `Task.Run`, etc.) or by making methods asynchronous with `async`/`await`. These approaches are usually safer and take care of details like thread management and exception propagation.

- **Use concurrent collections:** Replace manual locking logic around lists or dictionaries with concurrent collections wherever possible. For example, use `ConcurrentDictionary<int, string>` instead of a `Dictionary<int, string>` protected by your own lock. This reduces code complexity and the chance of bugs.

- **Profile your application:** Use built-in diagnostic tools (Visual Studio Diagnostics, `dotnet-counters`, or PerfView) to understand contention or bottlenecks. Look for areas with frequent locking, contention on shared resources, or long wait times for threads.

- **Use non-blocking algorithms:** If possible, use non-blocking patterns and data structures that permit high concurrency without requiring threads to be "paused" on locks for long periods. This helps scalability under heavy load.

- **Choose primitives wisely:** For simple critical section protection, a lock is enough. For high frequency reads and rare writes, use `ReaderWriterLockSlim`. For throttling or limiting resource usage, `SemaphoreSlim` is a good fit.

- **Leverage parallel LINQ (PLINQ):** For data processing tasks that can be parallelized, PLINQ is now more efficient due to runtime enhancements.

- **Use async/await everywhere:** On I/O-bound scenarios, such as file or network access, use `async/await` so that threads aren't wasted waiting for results.

Example Using `Parallel.For` for Concurrent Computation

```
Parallel.For(0, 100, i => {
    ProcessItem(i);
});
```

And with concurrent collections:

```
var bag = new ConcurrentBag<int>();
Parallel.For(0, 100, i => {
    bag.Add(i * i);
});
```

By using these practices and primitives, developers can make the most of modern hardware with minimal manual synchronization code, building applications that scale well on today's multi-core processors.

SIMD and Vectorization Improvements

AVX10.2 and SIMD Enhancements

Support for New Vector Instructions

.NET 10 significantly improves its SIMD (*single instruction, multiple data*) capabilities by adding support for the Advanced Vector Extensions 10.2 (AVX10.2) instruction set on x64 processors. AVX10.2 introduces wider and more versatile vector operations, allowing the platform to process more data in parallel using hardware-accelerated instructions. With these enhancements, developers now have access to a broader range of intrinsics through the new `System.Runtime.Intrinsics.X86.Avx10v2` class.

While hardware with AVX10.2 support is not yet widely available, .NET 10 lays the groundwork by incorporating the necessary JIT compiler logic and initial API surface. As new CPUs supporting AVX10.2 arrive, .NET 10 applications will be able to leverage the full suite of SIMD instructions seamlessly.

AVX10.2 includes the following improvements:

- Broader support for 256-bit and 512-bit wide SIMD instructions.

- Enhanced instruction sets for floating-point and integer operations.

- Lower abstraction overhead for mathematical, cryptographic, and AI scenarios.

- Improved compatibility with next-generation hardware, making .NET future-proof for developers.

Impact on Numerical Computing and Image Processing Workloads

The addition of AVX10.2 and expanded SIMD support has a direct and significant impact on workloads such as numerical computing, graphics, and image processing. Operations that process large arrays or perform repetitive computations, like matrix multiplications, vector additions, and image filters, benefit the most because more data can be processed simultaneously.

Benefits for developers:

- **Faster mathematical calculations:** This leads to massive speedups for libraries that use vector operations for tasks like matrix algebra, Fourier transforms, and convolutional filters.

- **AI, ML, and scientific workloads:** There is improved performance for AI libraries (such as ML.NET) due to more efficient processing of tensors and large data structures.

- **Graphics and image processing:** Operations such as color adjustments, blurring, and rescaling can be performed more efficiently, leading to smoother apps and faster image handling.

Sample Use Case: Vectorized Addition

```
using System.Numerics;

void AddVectors(float[] a, float[] b, float[] result)
{
    int i = 0;
    int simdLength = Vector<float>.Count;
    for (; i <= a.Length - simdLength; i += simdLength)
    {
        var va = new Vector<float>(a, i);
        var vb = new Vector<float>(b, i);
        (va + vb).CopyTo(result, i);
    }
    for (; i < a.Length; i++)
        result[i] = a[i] + b[i];
}
```

With AVX10.2 and improved JIT compilation, this code can execute more efficiently, utilizing new processor instructions without further code changes by the developer.

Enhanced Metrics APIs

Modern .NET development is all about understanding how your application runs in real time. To make this easier, .NET 10 brings important improvements to its runtime metrics APIs. These new tools help you get deep insights about garbage collection (GC) activity, thread pool usage, and method tiering, all as your app is running.

GC Insights

Garbage collection is normally hidden from day-to-day coding, but unexpected pauses or high memory usage often come back to how the GC behaves. .NET 10 expands what you can see through metrics APIs:

- **`GC.GetMemoryInfo()`:** This API gives details about heap structure, region sizes, fragmentation levels, and allocation history. It helps you spot memory leaks or premature promotion of objects to the large object heap.

- **Real-time metrics:** With performance tools, you can watch collections per second, time in GC, pause durations, and memory growth.

Example: Getting Heap Info

```
var info = GC.GetMemoryInfo();
Console.WriteLine($"Heap fragments: {info.FragmentedBytes}");
Console.WriteLine($"Total heap size: {info.HeapSizeBytes}");
```

These values can alert you to fragmentation before it becomes a problem.

Thread Pool Insights

The *thread pool* is central to scalable app performance, managing background processing, parallel tasks, and I/O completion handling. .NET 10 equips developers with straightforward APIs to observe thread pool health in real time. You can check how many worker threads and I/O completion threads are currently available, quickly spot if all threads are busy, and identify queuing bottlenecks.

For example, to display the number of available threads, you would use this:

```
int worker, io;
ThreadPool.GetAvailableThreads(out worker, out io);
Console.WriteLine($"ThreadPool: {worker} worker threads available");
```

Pairing this real-time data with dashboard tools like `dotnet-counters` makes it simple to watch for sudden spikes or slowdowns, so you can react before users feel any delay.

Method Tiering Insights

Method tiering is a runtime capability that optimizes hot code dynamically. As methods become "hot," they can be recompiled at higher optimization levels. .NET 10 enhances how the runtime reports tiering events and enables developers to track which parts of their codebase are being re-tiered for better performance.

Developers can use diagnostics event subscriptions, such as with `EventListener` or diagnostics listeners, to catch real-time notifications when methods are upgraded or when tiered compilation significantly alters execution speed. This visibility helps diagnose unexpected slowdowns or changes in behavior after new releases.

Gathering Actionable Metrics During Execution

Collecting and acting on metrics during execution has never been easier. Command-line tools like `dotnet-counters` provide a live dashboard experience for monitoring garbage collection, JIT compilation, and thread pool usage. `dotnet-monitor` allows for on-demand collection of traces and memory dumps from running applications, supporting reactive debugging and long-term observability.

Additionally, .NET 10 now integrates seamlessly with open monitoring standards like OpenTelemetry, making it possible to export runtime metrics to popular platforms such as Prometheus or Grafana. Within Visual Studio, advanced diagnostic tools give rich context and visualization for developers wanting to analyze memory usage patterns, CPU activity, and thread pool health as they debug.

By regularly observing these metrics, developers ensure their applications remain efficient and responsive under real-world stress. Early detection of issues using enhanced metrics APIs empowers quick fixes and more reliable performance, supporting both large-scale cloud services and smaller desktop applications.

CHAPTER 8

EF Core and .NET Libraries

Introduction

Entity Framework Core (EF Core) and the constantly growing .NET base libraries
are not merely background information for anyone working with .NET today; rather,
they are vital resources that facilitate efficient, contemporary software development.
Understanding these libraries and, more importantly, staying up to date with their
evolution is a valuable advantage for anyone working on serious .NET projects, even
though they are not the only way to build applications on the platform.

Demystifying .NET Libraries and EF Core

With every significant release, .NET libraries, which can range from small utilities
to expansive frameworks, have expanded and developed. These libraries are made
to lessen developer effort and promote solid, clean code, whether you are reading a
file, authenticating users, working with text, or connecting to the cloud. An excellent
example is EF Core, which abstracts away tedious tasks like SQL dialects and schema
migrations while allowing .NET applications to store, retrieve, and manipulate data
using expressive, composable queries.

Staying Current: Why It Really Matters

Practically speaking, there can be a significant difference between using tools from the
past and those from the present. Older patterns and libraries may "just work," but newer
versions often offer significant performance improvements, easier-to-use APIs, and

© Kajetan Duszyński 2025
K. Duszyński, *.NET 10 Revealed*, https://doi.org/10.1007/979-8-8688-1889-9_8

support for features that were previously truly challenging. Making your applications faster, easier to maintain, and able to handle current problems like handling large-scale data or integrating with AI workloads is more important than trying to keep up with the waves of innovation in the .NET ecosystem.

It can be tempting for developers in their early careers to learn the "classics" and stick with them, but those who keep up with library updates soon find tools that can change the way problems are solved. Performance enhancements, simplified APIs, and new features in EF Core and the libraries are all part of .NET 10's mission to help teams do more with less. You can optimize your code and keep your project healthier and more future-proof when you know what is new and how to use it.

The Big Picture with .NET 10

In addition to fixing long-standing problems, the most recent round of changes rethinks the capabilities of software engineers. For instance, EF Core 10 brings new patterns that correspond with the quick development of data-driven applications, faster model startup times, and more intelligent database queries. Subtle yet effective changes can be found throughout the larger .NET libraries: better memory management, more user-friendly date and time handling, more vigilant security defaults, and diagnostic tools designed with contemporary observability in mind.

As you progress through this chapter, you will discover that following the development of EF Core and .NET libraries is more about recognizing and taking advantage of opportunities for improved performance, more understandable code, and more maintainable solutions than it is about learning how to memorize techniques. This is one of the most useful mindsets you can cultivate in the ever-evolving world of technology.

Entity Framework Core 10: Major New Features and Enhancements

EF Core 10 carries on the legacy of simplifying, speeding up, and clarifying .NET data access. Developers can now express complex data queries directly in C# and have confidence that they will translate to the database efficiently, thanks to improved LINQ support and intelligent SQL generation.

Discovering *LeftJoin* and *RightJoin*

The addition of the LeftJoin and RightJoin operators to LINQ queries is one of the most notable features of EF Core 10. Complex setups are no longer necessary to link related tables, particularly when not every item on one side matches.

Consider creating a small library application where you want to view a list of all the books and any reviews that may be available for each one. The code becomes straightforward and readable by humans with EF Core 10:

```
var booksWithReviews = await context.Books
    .LeftJoin(
        context.Reviews,
        book => book.Id,
        review => review.BookId,
        (book, review) => new
        {
            BookTitle = book.Title,
            Review = review != null ? review.Content : "No review"
        })
    .ToListAsync();
```

Even if there is not a review, every book is included in this sample. The new operator does exactly what you want it to do.

Even if the book is no longer available (perhaps it was deleted, but you keep reviews for audits), there are situations when you may care more about reviews and want to show their paired book details. This is where RightJoin is useful:

```
var reviewsWithBooks = await context.Reviews
    .RightJoin(
        context.Books,
        review => review.BookId,
        book => book.Id,
        (review, book) => new
        {
            BookTitle = book != null ? book.Title : "Unknown Book",
            ReviewContent = review.Content
        })
    .ToListAsync();
```

This approach keeps your intentions and logic clear to anyone reading your code.

Simpler LINQ Translations

Additionally, EF Core 10 improves the translation of a variety of LINQ expressions
to SQL, making previously challenging queries easier to write and more effective at
runtime.

Consider an app that allows, but does not require, an organizer for each event. You
need a list of all events with their organizers, with Unassigned displayed if no one is
attached:

```
var eventsWithOrganizers = await context.Events
    .LeftJoin(
        context.Organizers,
        e => e.OrganizerId,
        o => o.Id,
        (e, o) => new
        {
            EventName = e.Name,
            Organizer = o != null ? o.Name : "Unassigned"
        })
    .Where(result => result.Organizer == "Unassigned" || e.IsPublic)
    .ToListAsync();
```

Now, this familiar business scenario takes just a few clear lines, and EF Core
produces efficient SQL under the surface, no hacks or verbose code required.

Expanded Operator Support: *GroupBy* and Aggregates with Clean SQL

EF Core 10 expands support for aggregation patterns beyond joins, which greatly
strengthens summaries and analytics code. This example reports the number of reviews
for each book:

```
var reviewCounts = await context.Reviews
    .GroupBy(r => r.BookId)
    .Select(g => new
```

```
{
    BookId = g.Key,
    Count = g.Count()
})
.ToListAsync();
```

This is not only easy to write but also generates optimized SQL that directly matches the aggregation, so your app remains performant as data grows.

Why These Changes Matter

- **Clearer code:** Your LINQ now directly expresses relationships and business intent, with minimal boilerplate code.

- **Faster queries:** Improvements in translation mean less work for the developer and the database, so your app handles data-heavy workloads with ease.

- **More possibilities:** With fewer limits on which LINQ patterns are supported, beginners and pros alike can solve a richer set of problems using familiar C# constructs.

EF Core 10's improvements aren't just about new features, they represent a leap in how naturally .NET apps can work with relational data, making modern development clearer and more accessible than ever.

ExecuteUpdateAsync Improvements in EF Core 10

With a particular emphasis on the flexibility of the `ExecuteUpdateAsync` API, EF Core 10 further simplifies how developers carry out extensive updates against databases. Code is now safer and more expressive thanks to this release's increased support for new scenarios and improved control over update specification and optimization.

A More Flexible Pattern for Bulk Updates

In the past, using EF Core to update records in bulk frequently required loading entities into memory, making changes to each one individually, and then saving the changes, an inefficient method for big datasets. With the advent and ongoing development of `ExecuteUpdateAsync`, developers can now update numerous records in the database without having to first retrieve them.

This approach becomes even more flexible in EF Core 10. With a single database command, you can specify multiple fields to update simultaneously and only target entities that meet a specific condition. Here's how simple and straightforward the solution becomes if you are running a retail application and want to offer a 10% discount to every product in a specific category:

```
await context.Products
    .Where(p => p.Category == "Clearance")
    .ExecuteUpdateAsync(setters => setters
        .SetProperty(p => p.Price, p => p.Price * 0.9)
        .SetProperty(p => p.LastDiscounted, _ => DateTime.UtcNow));
```

This code updates all products on clearance in one efficient step, sending only the necessary update command to the database, saving both memory and time.

Expression vs. Non-Expression Lambda Parameter Support

Another noteworthy improvement in EF Core 10 is the way `ExecuteUpdateAsync` handles lambda expressions. In previous versions, update logic had to be specified using expression lambdas (i.e., `Expression<Func<T, TValue>>`), which was required for accurate SQL translation but occasionally felt constrictive.

Both expression and non-expression (regular) lambda parameters are now more widely supported. This results in simpler, easier-to-read code by allowing you to use more natural, succinct lambdas in situations where SQL translation is not required. For instance, you can update properties with static values or supply default values without the need for additional boilerplate code:

```
await context.Orders
    .Where(o => o.Status == "Pending")
    .ExecuteUpdateAsync(setters => setters
        .SetProperty(o => o.Status, _ => "Processed")
        .SetProperty(o => o.ProcessedAt, _ => DateTime.UtcNow));
```

Here, `Status` and `ProcessedAt` are both updated for all pending orders, using non-expression lambdas for static assignment and timestamps. The flexibility to mix and match lambda types enables developers to write code that best matches the scenario, with EF Core 10 handling details behind the scenes.

Practical Benefits

The enhancements made to `ExecuteUpdateAsync` in EF Core 10 go beyond simple technical changes; they have a direct impact on how programmers write reliable and effective code. This API enables changes to thousands of records in a fraction of the time and complexity needed by conventional methods by running updates directly against the database. Imagine running a rapidly expanding e-commerce website where prices need to be changed or order statuses change all at once. EF Core 10 makes these tasks quick and eliminates the need to load each record into application memory. This makes high-volume tasks feasible even for those who are new to .NET, as it not only expedites routine maintenance but also lessens the resource load on your application.

The fact that these improvements maintain a gradual learning curve while still allowing for professional development is another significant advantage. You can read, write, and reason about your update logic with the same confidence and style that you use for other LINQ operations because the API was created with clarity in mind. As you get used to it, you will see how the flexibility of lambda support makes your code even more expressive and concise. You can easily update a property with a dynamically calculated value or a simple static value using patterns you already know.

Equally important, EF Core 10 allows you to concentrate on your main application logic by managing a lot of the complexities and pitfalls that occur behind the scenes. As your projects grow, you will produce cleaner, more consistent results because there will not be as many chances for errors like inadvertent data loading or embarrassing translation errors. Essentially, regardless of your level of experience, these useful benefits enable you to accomplish more with less code and less uncertainty.

Enhanced Azure Cosmos DB Integration in EF Core 10

Working with Azure Cosmos DB with EF Core 10 is more like an extension of regular .NET development than it is like battling a new paradigm. The most recent enhancements offer real chances to develop applications that require strong search capabilities, cutting-edge AI-driven insights, and smooth expansion as your data structures change. This section examines these characteristics, each supported by useful examples drawn from actual situations.

Unlocking Powerful Search: Full-Text Capabilities

Think about creating an internal messaging app for a remote team, where users can save everything from brainstorming logs to daily memos. No matter how much content is available, a teammate who is desperately looking for notes on an impending release expects results to be quick and pertinent.

With EF Core 10's full-text search support for Cosmos DB, you can enable users to instantly sift through thousands of records using their own words or phrases:

```
// Retrieve all project notes that mention "international launch"
var matchingMemos = await context.ProjectNotes
    .Where(note => EF.Functions.FullTextContains(note.Content,
    "international launch"))
    .ToListAsync();
```

This snippet gives back notes filled with valuable context, regardless of how scattered or informal the language might be. Your users get responses that are timely and tailored, transforming static data into a living, searchable resource.

Smarter Discovery: Hybrid and Vector Similarity Search with RRF

To advance your platform, consider incorporating intelligent document discovery. Suppose you are building a digital library where users want to find related research not only by keywords but also by conceptual or contextual similarity.

Reciprocal Rank Fusion (RRF) in EF Core 10 allows you to combine keyword-based and vector-based results instead of returning items that match a query word-for-word. By presenting articles or content pieces that match a user's intent, even when their query is vague or complex, this hybrid search gives your application an almost prescient feel.

```
// A vector produced by an AI model representing the user's search
intention
float[] queryVector = { 0.25f, 0.88f, 0.39f };

// Retrieve top documents by blending text relevance and vector proximity
var relevantArticles = await context.Articles
    .OrderBy(article => EF.Functions.Rrf(
```

```
    EF.Functions.FullTextScore(article.Text, "cloud security"),
    EF.Functions.VectorDistance(article.SemanticEmbedding, queryVector)))
  .Take(7)
  .ToListAsync();
```

Your app doesn't just answer questions; it recognizes intent, context, and nuance, making every query smarter and every result more helpful.

Growing Without Pain: Effortless Model Evolution and Default Values

As your application grows, so do its data models. But in many NoSQL setups, adding required fields can lead to frustrating compatibility problems. Legacy records might lack the new field, leading to runtime errors or unpredictable results.

EF Core 10 smooths this process by ensuring that when a record doesn't have a newly required property, a sensible default is automatically used. Think about launching a new user onboarding workflow: you add OnboardingStatus to profiles, but your system already has hundreds of users that were created before this feature existed. With this upgrade, there's no stress:

```
public class TeamMember
{
    public string Name { get; set; }
    public string OnboardingStatus { get; set; } = "NotStarted";
}

// When querying, existing members without this property are safely
assigned "NotStarted"
var newHires = await context.TeamMembers
    .Where(m => m.OnboardingStatus == "NotStarted")
    .ToListAsync();
```

Legacy users are automatically included in onboarding reports, and you don't need to run complex scripts or manually fix records. Development moves forward, uninterrupted.

For developers working on modern .NET applications, EF Core 10's integration with Azure Cosmos DB opens up a new level of functionality and ease. You now have a single toolkit that naturally supports all of these needs from within your regular code, eliminating the need to treat data search, model evolution, and intelligent recommendations as distinct engineering efforts.

Your user experience is completely changed by full-text search, which makes knowledge retrieval both intuitive and blazingly quick by making it easy to sort through large collections with just a natural language query. Hybrid search features, which combine the simplicity of keyword matching with the nuance of AI-powered semantic search, come into play as your dataset expands and user expectations rise. Users can now find connections that would otherwise be nearly impossible to find, thanks to your applications' ability to surface content that matches both what they typed and what they meant.

However, the advantages extend beyond search. One of the most persistent problems in NoSQL database design is addressed by EF Core 10, which silently manages the changing nature of application models. Model changes stop being a hassle by making sure that default values are automatically generated for missing fields. This implies that you will not have to worry about destroying current data or implementing laborious migration scripts as you iterate on your product, add new features, and address user feedback.

This most recent release is notable not only for its technical capabilities but also for the way these features work together to support the demands of rapid development and deployment. Whether you want to create focused internal applications or ambitious cloud platforms, you can now deliver smarter searches, maintain flexible data structures, and provide a user experience that feels intelligent and fast. The Cosmos DB integration improvements in EF Core 10 perfectly capture the spirit of.NET: take sophisticated, cutting-edge functionality and make it accessible, even for novices. As markets and technologies continue to change, this unified strategy promotes experimentation, expedites feature delivery, and gives developers the confidence to take on new challenges.

General Query and Performance Enhancements in EF Core 10

Entity Framework Core 10 introduces a number of useful enhancements that speed up and simplify common queries, particularly for operations involving types like `DateOnly` and `TimeOnly`, as well as for situations requiring pagination or extensive aggregation. This section examines each development to see how it can improve your applications.

Smarter Query Translation for *DateOnly* and *TimeOnly*

In contrast to the overloaded `DateTime` and `TimeSpan` types, the introduction of `DateOnly` and `TimeOnly` in recent .NET versions gave developers clearer semantics and decreased the likelihood of bugs. Building on this, EF Core 10 can now understand and translate logic involving these types directly in your queries.

Say you have a scheduling application that uses both `DateOnly` and `TimeOnly` to filter events that occur on a given date and after a specific time:

```
DateOnly targetDate = DateOnly.FromDateTime(DateTime.Today);
TimeOnly startTime = new TimeOnly(14, 0); // 2:00 PM

var lateAfternoonEvents = await context.Events
    .Where(e => e.EventDate == targetDate && e.StartTime > startTime)
    .ToListAsync();
```

In EF Core 10, this query is directly translated into SQL without any awkward workarounds, making your intent clear and your code safer. There's no need for manual conversions or type mismatches, the translation "just works," even for filtering and projections.

Optimized Handling of Limit and Count Operations

Efficient pagination and summary operations are vital for good app performance, especially when dealing with long lists or dashboards. EF Core 10 refines how it handles queries that chain `.Take()` (or `LIMIT`) and `.Count()` reduce unnecessary round-trips and leverage the underlying database optimally.

Consider an admin panel where you want to show a preview list of users along with the total count for quick stats:

```
int previewLimit = 5;

var previewUsers = await context.Users
    .OrderBy(u => u.Username)
    .Take(previewLimit)
    .ToListAsync();

var totalUsers = await context.Users.CountAsync();
```

Behind the scenes, EF Core 10 ensures that each query stays lightweight and efficient. When chaining further operations (e.g., Take().CountAsync()), it keeps the translation minimal, avoiding double-fetching or loading unnecessary data.

Support for String Functions with *char* Arguments

EF Core 10 now simplifies using string-related database functions that take a single character as an argument. This is particularly useful for tasks like filtering usernames by their starting letter or searching for a delimiter within a string.

Suppose you want to get all the usernames that start with the letter R:

```
char startingChar = 'R';

var usersStartingWithR = await context.Users
    .Where(u => u.Username.StartsWith(startingChar.ToString()))
    .ToListAsync();
```

Or, say that you're splitting address fields and need to check if a comma exists:

```
char delimiter = ',';

var withExtraInfo = await context.UserAddresses
    .Where(addr => addr.FullAddress.Contains(delimiter))
    .ToListAsync();
```

With EF Core 10, such filters use the character directly—no manual casting or string hacks required—leading to more readable code and optimized queries.

Performance Improvements for *MIN*, *MAX*, and *DISTINCT*

Aggregation and de-duplication are at the heart of reporting and analytics dashboards. EF Core 10 makes substantial improvements to how it translates and executes queries involving `MIN`, `MAX`, and `DISTINCT`. These now use more concise SQL and avoid fetching excess data.

Suppose you want to quickly show the range of order totals for the week and all the unique customer cities:

```
DateOnly weekStart = DateOnly.FromDateTime(DateTime.Today.AddDays(-7));

var minOrder = await context.Orders
    .Where(o => o.OrderDate >= weekStart)
    .MinAsync(o => o.TotalAmount);

var maxOrder = await context.Orders
    .Where(o => o.OrderDate >= weekStart)
    .MaxAsync(o => o.TotalAmount);

var customerCities = await context.Customers
    .Select(c => c.City)
    .Distinct()
    .ToListAsync();
```

In EF Core 10, these operations leverage improved query translation and avoid pulling unnecessary columns or records. The result? Faster response times and less load on your database server, even as your data grows.

These general query and performance upgrades in EF Core 10 remove much of the friction of previous versions, letting even beginner developers write clearer, more maintainable code, with the confidence that performance will keep up as their applications scale.

Usability and API Updates in EF Core 10

EF Core 10 introduces thoughtful changes aimed at making the development experience more intuitive and safe. Each improvement, whether it's about clearer SQL queries, stronger data protection, or more approachable configuration patterns, means your code is easier to write, read, and maintain, even as a beginner.

Simplified Naming for Generated SQL Query Parameters

In order to safely include your filter or update values into SQL commands sent to the database, EF Core uses parameters when building queries. In earlier iterations, these parameter names might have become obscure or difficult to follow in logs and diagnostics tools, particularly as queries became more complex.

The parameter names that EF Core 10 produces now closely match the variable or property that is being used in your LINQ expressions. In addition to being purely aesthetic, this clarity is very beneficial when examining audit logs or troubleshooting sluggish queries. For example, descriptive names like @Price or @Category will be used in place of confusing parameter names like @p1, making it much simpler to determine which value went where.

As an example, imagine you're debugging a sales dashboard and see this SQL in your logs:

```
SELECT * FROM Products WHERE Price > @Price
```

Now, you immediately know what the parameter represents and how it relates to the source code. This helps both with troubleshooting and when asking for help from colleagues, because everyone is literally speaking the same language—your code's language.

New Features for Logging and Sensitive Data Redaction

As .NET applications grow, so does the need to monitor what's happening inside them while protecting private data. EF Core 10 raises the bar for built-in diagnostics and privacy:

- **Improved logging:** The latest updates allow finer control over what gets logged, including easier filtering of specific command types or events. For example, you can choose to log just failed queries or only those that affect a certain table, cutting down on unnecessary noise.

- **Sensitive data redaction:** Perhaps even more importantly for beginners (who might miss subtle security pitfalls), EF Core now provides better mechanisms to ensure that sensitive values, like emails, passwords, and personal identifiers, are never exposed in logs by default. Suppose you turn on detailed SQL tracing during a support call; EF Core 10 ensures that actual values are automatically masked, reducing the risk of leaking confidential information. You can still enable detailed diagnostics in strictly controlled environments, but there's now solid protection by default.

For example, if you log a failed login attempt, instead of exposing actual emails or passwords in logs:

```
Login failed for user: *** (email hidden)
```

this makes your logs safer to share and archive, lowering compliance headaches for organizations.

Updates to Model Configuration Patterns

Model configuration, the process of telling EF Core how your C# entities map to database tables and columns, is now even more streamlined and approachable. EF Core 10 refines its "fluent" configuration APIs so you can describe more with less code.

- **Clearer chaining:** Configuration methods can now be chained more naturally, combining constraints and value conversions in a single, fluent line.

- **Less boilerplate code:** Many common configuration options now have sensible defaults, allowing you to omit repetitive setup unless you actually want custom behavior.

- **Modular setup:** EF Core 10 also supports breaking configuration into smaller, focused chunks. This means, for example, you can organize all date-related settings or indexes for a single entity in one place and all relationship rules in another, boosting code clarity.

For example, suppose you're setting up a `Task` entity. With modern conventions, your configuration might look like this:

```
modelBuilder.Entity<Task>(task =>
{
    task.Property(t => t.Title)
        .HasMaxLength(200)
        .IsRequired()
```

```
        .HasDefaultValue("New Task"); // All in one chain

    task.Property(t => t.CreatedAt)
        .HasDefaultValueSql("GETDATE()");
});
```

If you need more advanced behavior, you can easily move that configuration into a separate class, keeping your context clean and easy to navigate.

Advanced Performance and Compiled Models in EF Core 10

The time it takes for EF Core to boot up and prepare for work can become noticeable as your applications expand and your data models become more complex, particularly in serverless functions or cloud environments where every millisecond matters. Without requiring extensive knowledge or hours of manual tuning, EF Core 10 offers compiled models and new tooling to help make application starts almost instantaneous and improve runtime efficiency.

Compiling EF Core Models for Faster Startup

Every time an EF Core-powered app starts, it builds up an internal representation of your data model (the connections between .NET classes and database tables, columns, relationships, etc.). For small applications, this process is barely noticeable. For larger apps, or in scenarios where the application shuts down and starts frequently, like web APIs on demand, it can add a delay your users might feel.

Compiled models in EF Core 10 solve this by shifting the majority of model-building work from application startup to your development or build time. Instead of generating the model at runtime, you generate precompiled code files (or assemblies) as part of your regular build. When your app runs, it loads a model that's already ready, which dramatically reduces startup time and eliminates some parts of runtime overhead.

For example, say you have a complex e-commerce database with dozens of related entities. Enabling compiled models lets your application boot up and become responsive in seconds, rather than waiting for EF Core to piece everything together from scratch each time. This improvement is essential for highly scalable APIs, background jobs, and microservice architectures.

Using the *dbcontext optimize* Tooling

The new `dbcontext optimize` command is designed to make compiling your model a straightforward, beginner-friendly process,. No deep EF Core internals are required. Here's a simple step-by-step workflow any developer can follow:

1. Add the tools:

    First, install the EF Core command-line tools if you haven't already:

    ```
    dotnet tool install --global dotnet-ef
    ```

2. Run the `optimize` command:

    In your project folder (where your `dbcontext` is defined), run:

    ```
    dotnet ef dbcontext optimize
    ```

    This command analyzes your `dbcontext` and generates the necessary precompiled code files directly in your project.

3. Reference the compiled model:

    Make sure your application's startup code is updated to use the compiled model, usually by tweaking your `DbContextOptions` configuration. In most cases, EF Core will detect and use the optimized files automatically.

4. Rebuild your project:

    Rebuild your application as you normally would. Now, your app launches faster, and you're ready to deploy with confidence.

You don't have to manually edit or maintain the compiled code. Whenever your model changes (new properties, new relationships), simply repeat the `dbcontext optimize` command to refresh the precompiled model.

Why These Performance Gains Matter

Faster startup times are especially valuable for APIs running in cloud environments, on-demand functions, or for end-user desktop apps where perceived speed sets the tone for quality. Compiled models also mean less CPU use during application warm-up, which can reduce hosting costs and free up resources for actual business logic. This lets you focus on feature-building, knowing your ORM isn't quietly adding startup lag behind the scenes.

Core .NET 10 Libraries: What's New Across the Board

Dates, strings, sorting, data structures, and numerical computations are just a few of the carefully considered improvements to the base libraries that come with the release of .NET 10. These updates demonstrate Microsoft's continuous efforts to reduce resource consumption, make common programming patterns more expressive and potent, and make difficult tasks easier for novices.

ISOWeek Now Supports *DateOnly*: Precision for Week-Based Calculations

Traditionally, the ISOWeek class only used DateTime. Because so many current apps track "week of year" calculations, scheduling, payrolls, and weekly reporting, it was a pain to not be able to use the lighter DateOnly type. Finally, .NET 10 fills this gap. You can now use DateOnly directly to retrieve the ISO week and ISO year, or create a specific date based on the year, week number, and day. This implies that when working with date-only data in your apps, you will have less conversion code, fewer bugs, and more accurate logic.

```
DateOnly today = DateOnly.FromDateTime(DateTime.Now);
int week = ISOWeek.GetWeekOfYear(today);
DateOnly startOfWeek = ISOWeek.ToDateOnly(today.Year, week,
DayOfWeek.Monday);
```

String Normalization for Spans: Faster Text Processing, Fewer Allocations

String normalization is essential when you need to compare, store, or search text in a consistent way, even when characters have different binary representations (é versus e and an accent). Older .NET APIs only worked with entire strings, slowing down performance and increasing memory use when dealing with slices or spans. .NET 10 addresses this by introducing normalization APIs that work directly with ReadOnlySpan<char> and Span<char>. This means you can now normalize substrings, buffer data, or data in memory-mapped files with zero unnecessary copying or allocations, which is a big win for high-performance or real-time scenarios.

```
ReadOnlySpan<char> rawData = stackalloc char[] { 'e', '\u0301' };
// 'e' + combining accent
bool isNormalized = rawData.IsNormalized();
```

Numeric Ordering for String Comparison: Sorting That Makes Sense

Sorting version numbers or filenames naturally has long been a hassle. Lexicographic sorting would mistakenly rank file10 before file2, even though ten comes after two. .NET 10 introduces numeric-aware string comparers: just enable the NumericOrdering flag and your string sorting will finally follow human intuition. This is particularly useful for UIs, data processing, or any scenario where natural/human ordering is required.

```
var comparer = StringComparer.Create(System.Globalization.CultureInfo.
CurrentCulture, System.Globalization.CompareOptions.NumericOrdering);

List<string> versions = new() { "v2", "v10", "v1" };
versions.Sort(comparer); // Results in: v1, v2, v10
```

More Expressive Overloads for *OrderedDictionary* and *DateTime*

For data structures, OrderedDictionary<TKey, TValue> in .NET 10 now supports overloads that provide the index of keys when adding or retrieving values. This lets you combine the fast lookup of dictionaries with precise ordering control, essential for scenarios like tracking game scores, user inputs, or anything needing both order and direct access.

```
OrderedDictionary<string, int> scores = new();
if (!scores.TryAdd("Alice", 10, out int index))
{
    scores.SetAt(index, scores.GetAt(index).Value + 5);
}
```

For `DateTime`, new overloads increase flexibility and make it easier to construct or modify date-time objects concisely, supporting a wide array of calendar and time operations, especially helpful for localized or time zone-aware calculations.

Updates to *TimeSpan.FromMilliseconds*

Earlier versions forced you to use an overload of `TimeSpan.FromMilliseconds` with an optional microseconds argument, which could trip up tools like LINQ that don't handle optional parameters well. .NET 10 introduces a dedicated single-parameter overload, making the method easier to use in queries and code generation. Now, expressing precise durations, like a timeout of `1200 milliseconds`, fits naturally into LINQ expressions and lambda-based APIs.

```
TimeSpan delay = TimeSpan.FromMilliseconds(1200);
// Clear, concise, and now always supported
```

Enhancements for Matrix Transformation Methods

In fields like graphics, 3D games, or simulations, matrix transformations are fundamental. .NET 10 adds left-oriented versions of matrix-creation methods for billboard and constrained billboard matrices. For developers working with left-oriented coordinate systems, this means physics, animation, and graphics computations now match the conventions of many 3D engines and mathematical libraries, eliminating confusion and making integration smoother.

```
var billboard = Matrix4x4.CreateBillboardLeftHanded(objectPos, cameraPos,
upVec, forwardVec);
```

Performance and Memory Improvements in .NET 10

.NET 10 delivers a range of enhancements aimed directly at core library performance, helping applications go faster, use less memory, and minimize resource usage in scenarios that matter most to new and seasoned developers alike. These improvements touch critical areas such as file archiving, array handling, and routine data processing, bringing smoother resource management and lower overhead to everyday tasks.

ZipArchive: Faster, Leaner File Compression and Extraction

File archiving with `ZipArchive` is a common task, whether it's exporting database backups, packaging project logs, or sharing documents. In earlier .NET versions, updating files inside existing ZIP archives often required loading every entry into memory, resulting in slow performance and heavy RAM consumption, especially with large files.

With .NET 10, major improvements arrive:

- **Optimized update mode:** When you add or replace files in a ZIP archive, only the modified files are processed and written, rather than the entire archive. This change leads to dramatically lower memory usage and almost instantaneous updates, even for massive archives.

- **Parallelized extraction:** Decompressing ZIP files is now much faster, thanks to internal adjustments that allow for parallel processing. You'll notice that extraction completes sooner and with smaller memory footprints, particularly when working with large or many files.

For example, processing an archive containing several gigabytes, such as app logs or bulk exports, sees updates that are over 99% faster and with a fraction of the memory use.

Stack Allocation for Small Arrays: Lightning Fast, Zero Garbage

Stack allocation is a longstanding performance technique for temporary or short-lived data, traditionally applied only to individual value types. .NET 10 extends this power to entire small arrays, even for reference types.

- **Small value-type arrays:** If you need a handful of integers, floats, or structs for a quick computation or buffer, they're now allocated on the stack rather than the heap, eliminating garbage collection overhead.

- **Small reference-type arrays:** Arrays holding a few object references (like a small pool of strings or temp results) are also stack-allocated if their use doesn't outlast the current method.

For example, if you create a small buffer for image processing or a temporary scratch space for parsing, the underlying array is stack-allocated by the JIT compiler. This means much faster allocation and no burden on the garbage collector, so your app remains responsive even under heavy mini-batch workloads.

```
// Quick math buffer ,  auto stack-allocated if small and scoped
int[] weights = {1, 2, 3};
int result = weights.Sum();
```

Array Interface and Enumeration Optimizations: Minimal Abstraction, Maximal Speed

Enumerating arrays (especially via LINQ, `IEnumerable`, or generic collection interfaces) is a foundation of .NET coding. In past versions, using an array through an interface could add significant overhead, because the JIT compiler had trouble removing the extra layers of abstraction, leading to slower loops and more memory pressure.

.NET 10 introduces array interface method devirtualization and enumeration deabstraction:

- **Devirtualization:** The JIT can now recognize common array operations (such as `foreach` or LINQ calls that hide the array type behind an interface) and optimize them down to direct, index-based loops.

- **Performance gains:** The penalty for looping through an array via
  `IEnumerable` has dropped from 83% overhead in .NET 9 to around
  10% in .NET 10, nearly matching direct array access for most
  workloads.

Consider this example:

```
// Whether looping directly or through IEnumerable, performance is nearly
the same now
IEnumerable<int> numbers = new int[] {3, 1, 4, 1, 5};
int total = 0;
foreach (var num in numbers)
    total += num;
```

You can confidently use interfaces, LINQ, and other familiar patterns with arrays, knowing that .NET 10 keeps your code beautiful and blazing fast.

Diagnostics, Observability, and Telemetry in .NET 10

The advances in diagnostics and observability in .NET 10 make it easier than ever to track, understand, and optimize modern applications. From enhanced telemetry capabilities to better alignment with open standards, these updates help beginners and experienced developers keep their apps reliable and insightful.

Telemetry Schema URL Support in ActivitySource and Meter

Distributed systems rely on structured telemetry to trace operations and measure performance. In .NET 10, the `ActivitySource` and `Meter` APIs now directly support specifying a telemetry schema URL when you construct them. This schema URL provides a machine-readable contract describing the tracing or metrics structure your application produces, ensuring that all distributed tracing and telemetry data align with a known specification.

This means when your app emits telemetry, anyone who consumes the data (internally or via observability tools) can automatically interpret it correctly, helping streamline integration with monitoring platforms or partner services.

For example, say you want to create a custom activity source for tracking API requests and specify a schema for your trace:

```
var activitySource = new ActivitySource(
    new ActivitySourceOptions("MyApiService")
    {
        Version = "1.0.0",
        TelemetrySchemaUrl = "https://example.com/schemas/api-traces/v1"
    });

var meter = new Meter("MyApiService", "1.0.0", telemetrySchemaUrl:
"https://example.com/schemas/api-metrics/v1");
```

This setup means that every trace and metric generated can be validated, processed, or visualized according to your specified schema, helping maintain consistency as your system evolves.

Updates to Match OpenTelemetry Specifications

.NET 10 strengthens its alignment with the OpenTelemetry specification, the industry standard for collecting telemetry data. This includes:

- **Schema URL alignment:** Ensuring telemetry data is tagged and organized per OpenTelemetry's guidelines.

- **`ActivitySourceOptions` and `MeterOptions`:** New construction options simplify setup, help you set attributes like tags or schema URLs, and make configuration clearer.

- **Out-of-process trace support:** Improvements in serialization enable more complete trace data, including custom events and links, to be exported to external monitoring tools.

- **Rate-limit trace sampling:** New features allow for smarter trace collection, reducing noise and controlling telemetry costs.

These updates ensure that .NET telemetry integrates smoothly with popular observability tools, including Grafana, Jaeger, Prometheus, and cloud-based tracing platforms, without extra adapters or risky custom configurations. Developers adopting .NET 10 are set up for success with a solution that "just works" on modern infrastructure.

CHAPTER 9

Migration and Compatibility

Introduction

Making the switch to .NET 10 can be exciting and a little frightening if you are working with older code or have applications that are already in place. Understanding migration and compatibility is the first step to ensuring a smoother and more confident transition. This chapter discusses the significance of moving to .NET 10, what compatibility means in this context, and the goals you should keep in mind when doing so.

Why Migration Matters in .NET 10

There are other reasons to upgrade to a new version of .NET besides using the newest features. Migration is essential because it often leads to improved performance, enhanced security, and access to new APIs that can help you develop applications more quickly and intelligently. Because the development environment is always changing, updates may not always be available for older .NET versions. Upgrading your software will keep it safe from new security threats and supported. Additionally, as more individuals and organizations embrace the latest technologies, it becomes simpler to locate support, examples, and current libraries for your projects. Using out-of-date versions often leads to more work later on because things eventually break or become incompatible with new tools.

© Kajetan Duszyński 2025
K. Duszyński, *.NET 10 Revealed*, https://doi.org/10.1007/979-8-8688-1889-9_9

The Importance of Compatibility

Making sure your code continues to function as intended after the switch to .NET 10 is the main goal of compatibility. If other people depend on your software, you do not want to ruin what has already worked. Say you have a library that other programmers utilize. Everyone may experience issues if you upgrade to .NET 10 and it stops functioning. Compatibility lessens that danger. It implies that current features should remain functional or, in the event that they must be modified, should be transparent and thoroughly documented. Although .NET team makes every effort to maintain compatibility, there are always some changes when a major new version is released. You can more easily plan, test, and address any problems early if you know which areas are likely to break and why.

Key Migration and Compatibility Goals in .NET 10

The primary objectives for compatibility and migration with .NET 10 are obvious. The update's primary goal is to reduce breaking changes. This implies that your migration should be easier if you adhere to standard procedures and keep up with new releases. Offering unambiguous tools and documentation that assist you in identifying the changes before you even begin the upgrade is another objective. Additionally, .NET 10 aims to increase process predictability so that you do not waste time on unforeseen issues.

Last but not least, .NET 10 works to support a variety of platforms, including Windows, Linux, macOS, and various devices. In this manner, your code will function everywhere with less work on your part. In order to make the transition to .NET 10 beneficial for both you and your software, this chapter explains how to utilize these enhancements and what to look out for.

Understanding .NET 10: Overview for Migration

When you're getting ready to move your apps or libraries to .NET 10, it's helpful to have a broad understanding of what this new version brings, especially for developers making the transition from older versions of .NET. This section covers what's new in .NET 10 for migration scenarios, how support policies work with LTS (long-term support) and maintenance, and which platforms are supported, including updates to system requirements.

What's New in .NET 10 for Migration

A number of enhancements brought about by .NET 10 are intended to make migrations more dependable and seamless. The improved compatibility with earlier .NET versions is one significant update. During your migration, tools like the API Portability Analyzer and .NET Upgrade Assistant have been enhanced to detect more edge cases and give you more understandable feedback. Better diagnostics for detecting breaking changes are also introduced in .NET 10, which makes it simpler to identify and fix compatibility problems early.

Better support for modern project layouts, such as SDK-style projects, will also be apparent to you. When you're updating older projects, these make it easier to manage dependencies and organize your code. Updates have been made to NuGet's dependency handling, including compatibility checks to make sure third-party libraries are prepared for .NET 10. Furthermore, there are new APIs that simplify the process of moving legacy code to new patterns, which lessens the manual labor you may have previously encountered.

Additionally included in the package are performance enhancements. Faster startup times, more effective resource usage, and updates that improve the performance of your migrated projects on various hardware are all to be expected in .NET 10. Whether you are moving a small library or a large, complex solution, these changes provide you with a more predictable and guided experience.

LTS and Support Lifecycle

Knowing how long .NET 10 will be supported is essential when organizing your migration. LTS (long-term support) and STS (standard-term support) are the two primary tracks of the structured support lifecycle for .NET.

Since .NET 10 is an LTS release, security updates, bug fixes, and patches will be applied for a longer time frame, typically three years after the release date. This provides you with the assurance that your migrated apps will continue to be safe and supported for a predetermined period of time. Major updates can be planned less frequently with LTS, allowing you to prioritize stability and long-term planning over frequent, urgent upgrades.

Although minor versions receive frequent updates as well, most teams primarily expect reliable, stable builds during the LTS period. With Microsoft's explicit end-of-support dates, you can always anticipate when the next upgrade window will be available.

Supported Platforms and System Requirements

Your applications will function nearly anywhere thanks to .NET 10's continued support for a variety of platforms. You can target Linux, macOS, and Windows, and the most recent versions of each are supported. This wide compatibility also applies to ARM and x64 architectures, as well as containers like Docker.

Full support for Windows desktop technologies like Windows Forms and WPF, as well as cross-platform UI frameworks via .NET MAUI, are included in .NET 10 for desktop and mobile projects. Blazor and ASP.NET Core are equally supported on all major web platforms. Before migrating, make sure your servers and development computers meet the new standards, as the system requirements have also been updated to reflect the most recent OS versions.

Minimum requirements typically include modern CPUs and a recent version of the operating system, often Windows 10 or later, the latest versions of popular Linux distributions, and the current release of macOS. Memory and storage needs are like previous versions but keep in mind that new features and platform support are optimized for newer hardware and OS releases. Checking these requirements early helps you avoid surprises during your migration journey.

By understanding these essentials, you can plan and execute a .NET 10 migration with more confidence, knowing your apps will be faster, safer, and ready for the future.

Planning Your Migration

It is a big task to move your software to .NET 10, and planning each step can help you avoid issues later. This section walks you through the primary steps, which include assessing what you currently have, choosing a migration strategy, comprehending and managing risks, and utilizing tools that will facilitate your work.

Inventory and Assessment of Existing Applications

The best place to start is by attentively examining your current applications. Provide a list of every project you oversee, together with details about the frameworks and third-party libraries they use. Check to see if any of the components your apps depend on have changed or are no longer accessible in .NET 10. Provide details on operating system dependencies, file storage, database access, and any external APIs. This inventory will help you identify which projects can be shifted most readily and which ones need more work.

Choosing a Migration Strategy

Once you know what you have, you need to pick a migration strategy. Not all apps have to move at the same time or in the same way. You might decide to start with small, less risky projects. Or you could pick a critical app that will benefit most from new features and improved performance. The main idea is to match your approach to your team's skills, time, and business needs.

Full Migration vs. Incremental Migration

You switch to .NET 10 all at once when you do a full migration. This has the benefit of rapidly updating all of your projects and facilitates the adoption of new practices throughout your codebase. However, because a lot can change at once, this method can be dangerous for large or complex software.

One library, module, or application at a time, your code is moved in smaller steps with an incremental migration. In this manner, you can test and address problems as they arise without impacting the system as a whole. Because it distributes the risk and workload over time, incremental migration is typically appropriate for larger applications or businesses with numerous dependencies.

Risks and Mitigation Plans

Migration can present certain difficulties. Breaking changes in .NET 10, incompatible third-party libraries, and variations in runtime behavior are a few risks. Additionally, there might be undiscovered bugs that only become apparent after updating to the latest version.

Plan to maintain backups of your previous code, run your tests frequently, and use side-by-side builds to verify each step in order to mitigate these risks. Before you start, look into all dependencies for support of .NET 10. Create a rollback strategy for larger systems so you can go back to the earlier iteration if something goes wrong. Effective team communication also aids in identifying problems early.

Tools and Resources for Migrating to .NET 10

Several tools are available to make migration easier and help identify issues before they cause trouble:

- **.NET Upgrade Assistant:** The purpose of this tool is to assist you in upgrading a project to .NET 10. It replaces out-of-date APIs, updates dependencies, examines your project file, and indicates any areas that require manual modifications. Its step-by-step interface makes it suitable for a variety of project types, such as web projects, console apps, and libraries. You can find extensive description at `https://learn.microsoft.com/en-us/dotnet/core/porting/upgrade-assistant-overview`.

- **API Portability Analyzer:** The API Portability Analyzer determines which APIs in your project are compatible with .NET 10. It provides you with a useful report that identifies the APIs that may be problematic and indicates where you may need to modify your code or look for alternatives. Large codebases or older libraries that might not have updates benefit greatly from this. You can find extensive description at `https://learn.microsoft.com/en-us/dotnet/standard/analyzers/portability-analyzer`.

Using these tools, you can spot potential trouble areas before you start migrating, making the rest of the process quicker and less risky.

Breaking Changes in .NET 10

Knowing how breaking changes are handled and the various ways they could affect your code is crucial as you get ready to switch to .NET 10. In addition to offering straightforward definitions and examples of the various types you may come across, this section describes how these changes are monitored and categorized.

How Breaking Changes Are Documented and Categorized

Microsoft tracks and publishes all major breaking changes for .NET in a dedicated documentation section. Each change is grouped by technology area—such as ASP. NET Core, core libraries, or containers—and is carefully described. Each entry explains what's changed, which type of incompatibility is involved, and the version where it was introduced. The main categories used for breaking changes are:

- Binary incompatible

- Source incompatible

- Behavioral change

This classification helps you quickly assess the risk for your migration project and decide on the necessary remediation steps. In the official documentation, every breaking change is listed with practical information, code snippets, and guidance for adapting your code if necessary.

Binary Incompatibility

An existing compiled binary (DLL or EXE) that functioned in a previous version of .NET may no longer load or run properly in .NET 10. This is known as binary incompatibility. Even if the source has not changed, this frequently means you will need to recompile your code.

If a public type is deleted from a library or if the signature of a method is altered, binary incompatibilities can show up. For instance, even if you do not recompile an application that references a type that your application uses, it will not function on the new runtime if the library author removes or renames that type.

For instance, code compiled against an old version of a method that used to accept strings but now only accepts integers will not run unless it is recompiled and updated.

Source Incompatibility

Source incompatibility occurs when the source code will not compile successfully without modifications when recompiled using the most recent version of the .NET SDK or runtime target. This frequently occurs when APIs are changed, renamed, or removed in a way that makes the original code incompatible with the updated definition.

Compilation can be broken by modifications such as tighter API checks, the elimination of outdated APIs, or the updated overload resolution in C# 14. Your code will need to be modified to comply with the new regulations. When recompiling your application for .NET 10, you may encounter errors right away, even if there are no issues when using older binaries.

As an example, if your project contains a direct package reference, which the framework in .NET 10 now provides, the new warning NU1510 is raised. If you do not remove these references, the new SDK will cause your build to fail.

Behavioral Changes

A behavioral change happens when code behaves differently at runtime, even if it compiles and loads successfully. This might not require code updates, but the effect can be confusing or problematic if you rely on the old behavior.

Behavioral changes can include changes in how methods return data, how framework components interact, or defaults that are now different. For instance, adjustments in activity creation and tracing APIs, new default values for configuration, or runtime optimizations (like improved stack allocation) can all cause your app to function differently than it did before, even though it builds and runs.

As an example, in .NET 10, the way small arrays can be allocated on the stack (instead of the heap) improves performance but might also change subtle runtime behaviors in resource use or debugging.

Understanding these categories will make it easier to plan, test, and execute your migration to .NET 10 with fewer surprises and more confidence.

Migration from .NET Framework, .NET Core, and .NET 5–9

Adopting the newest developments and getting your apps ready for the future are key components of .NET 10 migration. Knowing the key distinctions between .NET 10 and earlier iterations, the special benefits you receive, and the difficulties with older technologies or large application architectures are all essential for doing this with confidence.

Differences Between .NET Framework and .NET 10

Platform support and flexibility are where .NET Framework and .NET 10 diverge most noticeably. While .NET 10 is cross-platform by design, .NET Framework has always been primarily focused on Windows. You can run your applications on Windows, Linux, and macOS with .NET 10, and the framework offers excellent support for containers. With frequent updates, fascinating new features, and improved performance, .NET 10 is being actively developed while .NET Framework is in maintenance mode and only receives security or compatibility fixes.

The organization and development of applications is another significant change. SDK-style projects are used in .NET 10, which simplifies configuration and enhances uniformity among libraries and apps. Code and packages can now be shared more readily across web, desktop, mobile, and cloud applications thanks to the unification of the base class libraries.

Key Benefits of Migrating from Older .NET Versions

There are several advantages to moving your code to .NET 10. The most recent runtime enhancements are instantly utilized by applications, which leads to quicker startup times and lower memory consumption. You can use a single codebase or collection of libraries to develop for multiple platforms with the unified SDK approach.

Another significant advantage is security; enhanced cryptography libraries and default support for contemporary security protocols in .NET 10 reduce the possibility of vulnerabilities. For mission-critical apps, long-term support provides peace of mind by ensuring regular fixes and updates for a number of years. Teams can work more efficiently and identify problems sooner with the help of new development tools like hot reload and advanced diagnostics.

Developers will also find it easier to integrate with DevOps practices. With .NET 10, containerization is fully supported and deployment pipelines become more predictable, speeding up delivery and testing.

Special Considerations for Legacy Technologies

Not all .NET Framework technologies are compatible with .NET 10. For instance, Web Forms are completely unsupported. You will need to switch to more recent web technologies like ASP.NET Core MVC or Blazor if your applications are based on Web Forms. These choices offer contemporary web development patterns in addition to comparable capabilities.

Another area that has changed is Windows Communication Foundation (WCF), which is not supported server-side in .NET 10. The suggested course of action is to use ASP.NET Core to switch to REST or gRPC APIs. Reusing current WCF clients can occasionally be facilitated by community projects and client libraries, but if you host WCF services today, you should expect some redesign.

.NET 10 does not support some other features, including application domains, remoting, and workflow services. Projects that rely on these will need to be handled more carefully, frequently refactoring or replacing whole functional sets.

Modernizing Architecture: Monolith to Microservices

Upgrading to .NET 10 offers you the opportunity to reconsider the design of your application in addition to being a technical process. Many businesses take advantage of the migration to start decomposing big, monolithic apps into more manageable, standalone microservices. Independent service design, deployment, and scaling are made simpler by .NET 10's support for containers, lightweight APIs, and robust cloud platform integration.

It is also more feasible to transition to a cloud-native strategy with .NET 10. Modern applications are easier to manage and more dependable, thanks to built-in features like logging, health checks, and configuration. Consistent project formats and cross-platform tools can help you make continuous integration, and delivery pipelines a standard component of your workflow.

Your applications will become more maintainable and scalable in the long run if you begin the modernization process with small, gradual steps, such as separating background processes or testing out new microservices for specific system components, even if you cannot completely revamp your application in a day.

In the end, updating to .NET 10 is a crucial step in maintaining the future-readiness of your software. Although there are actual difficulties with legacy systems, the advantages in terms of productivity, scalability, and security make the process worthwhile.

Updating Project Files and Dependencies

To fully benefit from .NET 10, it's important to update your project files and manage your dependencies with care. This helps avoid unexpected issues during migration and allows you to use all the latest features of the platform.

Moving to SDK-Style Projects

SDK-style projects are now the standard way to organize .NET projects. If you are using older project formats, converting to SDK style should be your first step. These project files are much simpler; they use `.csproj` files that are easier to read and manage. You usually need just a few lines to define your project, and adding or updating dependencies is much more straightforward. The new format also brings automatic file inclusion, better support for multi-targeting, and seamless integration with new build tools.

If you open an older project in a recent version of Visual Studio, you will often be prompted to upgrade it. Official migration tools and guides show exactly which lines to change or remove. Moving to SDK-style not only prepares your app for .NET 10, but also makes your workflow cleaner and more future-proof.

Target Framework Monikers (TFM) for .NET 10

When you upgrade, you must change the Target Framework Moniker (TFM) in your project file to signal that you're using .NET 10. This tells the compiler and build tools which version of the platform your app targets. In your `.csproj` file, you replace older values like `<TargetFramework>netcoreapp3.1</TargetFramework>` or `<TargetFramework>net5.0</TargetFramework>` with the new moniker for .NET 10: `<TargetFramework>net10.0</TargetFramework>`.

Setting the correct TFM ensures that you get access to new APIs, optimizations, and the latest support while keeping your builds consistent and up to date. If your library needs to work with multiple .NET versions, you can list several TFMs using `<TargetFrameworks>` and separate them with semicolons.

Upgrading NuGet Packages and Third-Party Dependencies

Additional libraries and functionality are provided by NuGet packages for your application; however, their compatibility with .NET 10 must also be verified. Start by using the dotnet CLI or your IDE to check for updates. The majority of package authors keep their versions up to date with the most recent .NET release; however, occasionally packages may not function properly with .NET 10 or are no longer supported. Examine each one, replacing unsupported packages with alternatives or updating to newer versions.

If internal or in-house libraries support multiple projects on various platforms, you may need to multi-target them or rebuild them against .NET 10. Upgrades should always be thoroughly tested, because even small adjustments to dependencies can have an impact on how an application behaves.

Dealing with Deprecated APIs

Older APIs are deprecated and occasionally removed in all major .NET releases, including .NET 10. Warnings about out-of-date methods or classes might appear when you build your project. Review these warnings and, if you can, change your code to utilize the suggested replacement APIs.

You can find deprecated APIs and propose alternative methods to accomplish the same goals with the aid of the migration analyzers and .NET documentation. By taking care of these now, you can improve the maintainability of your project and prevent future updates from breaking it. After making changes, spend some time thoroughly testing because the code may behave differently.

Maintaining your project files and dependencies up to date is essential to the success of your .NET 10 migration.

Migrating ASP.NET Applications

By moving your ASP.NET apps to .NET 10, you can benefit from the most recent security patches, performance enhancements, and framework updates. This section describes the latest developments in web APIs and OpenAPI 3.1 support, how the project structure and hosting model are changing, what has changed in the API surface, and how middleware and routing should be handled during a migration.

Changes in the ASP.NET API Surface

ASP.NET introduces new APIs, deprecates some older ones, and makes some radical shifts with .NET 10. Numerous low-level APIs have been expanded to cover more use cases or have been updated for clarity. For instance, new features for minimal APIs and advanced model binding have been added, and configuration and logging extensions have been enhanced.

In earlier iterations, certain APIs that were designated as obsolete have since been eliminated. After migrating, you may encounter compilation errors or warnings if your application uses outdated extension methods or has direct access to low-level HTTP handlers. Microsoft offers compatibility analyzers to assist you in identifying these problems early on and recommend suitable alternatives.

Updated Project Structure and Hosting Model

The SDK-style project file format is still used for ASP.NET Core `.csproj`, but .NET 10 promotes more explicit dependency management and even cleaner concern separation. The new templates emphasize clean, well-organized code and frequently use the newest features, such as top-level statements and implicit usings, to cut down on boilerplate code.

Additionally, hosting in .NET 10 is simplified. A more condensed setup, frequently based on top-level statements, is now used in the `Program.cs` file.

OpenAPI 3.1 and Other Web API Changes

More precise and detailed API descriptions are made possible by .NET 10's update of ASP.NET Core's support for OpenAPI (Swagger) documentation to version 3.1. More data types, enhanced validation, and better JSON Schema compatibility are all supported by OpenAPI 3.1. Make sure your documentation generators and API endpoints reflect these changes when you migrate. For complete compatibility with OpenAPI 3.1, some properties or configuration patterns used for OpenAPI 2.0 or 3.0 might need to be modified.

Additional modifications for web APIs include enhanced features in minimal APIs, better support for endpoint filters, and better validation attributes. Simplified endpoint definitions eliminate the need for separate controllers for basic APIs and enable you to write succinct handlers right in the route mapping.

Migration of Middleware and Routing

Middleware registration in .NET 10 remains familiar, but with some variations. Minimal APIs encourage you to use the builder pattern and register middleware in a more functional style. For instance, inline middleware can now be used with simple lambda expressions. While this is optional, it can lead to clearer, shorter application startup code.

Routing updates provide greater flexibility, including better route parameter binding and support for new endpoint filters. If your app relies on complex attribute routing or custom conventions, review the breaking change documentation to ensure compatibility.

During migration, double-check your middleware order and any custom middleware logic. Some interfaces and extension methods might have changed, and behavior could differ slightly, especially when moving you're from older ASP.NET versions where middleware signatures or expectations have evolved.

With careful review and by adopting new patterns as needed, you can take full advantage of the speed, maintainability, and features of .NET 10 in your ASP.NET projects.

Migrating Blazor, MAUI, and Other UI Technologies

Moving your app's user interface to .NET 10 can unlock cool new benefits and help you build for more devices with less code. Whether you use Blazor for web UIs, .NET MAUI for mobile or desktop, or other supported frameworks, it's worth knowing exactly what to expect during this upgrade, including some things that might trip you up if you're not watching closely.

Starting with Blazor, you'll notice that .NET 10 keeps developing this framework with fresh features and, of course, some changes that require your attention. One of the main things to check is how your components interact with their APIs. The lifecycle hooks and rendering patterns have seen some tweaks, making certain old setups and obsolete parameters no longer valid. The navigation system also gets smarter; routing now handles parameters and fallback routes with more consistency, and if your app relies on custom logic for moving between pages, you'll want to test and maybe adjust your code after switching versions.

Security and logins work a little differently, too. For Blazor WebAssembly apps in particular, .NET 10 adds updated flows for authentication, especially when you're connecting to third-party identity services or managing user sessions with ASP.NET Core

Identity. If your app relies on calling JavaScript code from C# and going back and forth, it's important to double-check those parts as well. Handling of async calls and error feedback can be slightly different, so you'll want to test interactions thoroughly.

If you're migrating a .NET MAUI application, there's a bit of housekeeping to do before the upgrade. First, you'll need to update the project files to use the latest SDK version and explicitly target .NET 10 in your configuration. This often involves editing the `csproj` file and making sure your settings line up with what the new system expects, such as `net10.0-ios`, `net10.0-android`, or other platform-specific targets. You'll also need to make sure your development tools—like Visual Studio, Xcode for iOS, and the Android SDK—are up to date, because .NET 10 relies on the newest versions.

Certain controls, platform features, or ways of handling platform-specific code may have changed or been phased out. If you were using custom renderers or effects before, look out for any replacements or handler-based approaches in the documentation. Also, .NET MAUI has refined how you add and name images, fonts, and other shared resources, making it easier for the app to use the same resources on every platform. You might need to move files and update some paths, which provides a good opportunity to make things tidier.

After you migrate, make a habit of running your app on every device you care about—Windows, Mac, Android, and iOS. Just because something works on one platform doesn't mean it behaves the same on all the others. You might notice small layout or interaction differences and need to tweak settings for a smooth user experience everywhere.

On a bigger scale, .NET 10 encourages you to write code that can run anywhere. Try following patterns like MVVM (Model-View-View-Model) or MVU (Model-View-Update) to keep the business logic separate from your UI details, which makes it much easier to share and test code. Building reusable components is highly recommended in both Blazor and MAUI, so you spend less time repeating yourself and more time shipping features. Remember to keep your layouts flexible, so your app still looks great whether it's running on a phone, tablet, desktop, or large display.

Finally, with MAUI's single project structure, you get one place to manage everything—shared code, resources, and platform-specific tweaks. This makes building and upgrading cross-platform apps a lot smoother, and it helps when your team grows or new devices come out.

Upgrading your UI projects to .NET 10 is actually a great time to review how you organize and design your app. Adopting the newest patterns and best practices doesn't just protect you from bugs and incompatibilities; it sets you up for faster updates and long-term success across every platform you want to reach.

Libraries, Packages, and Third-Party Integrations

Making sure your project's libraries and external integrations work well in .NET 10 is a crucial step in your migration journey. With each new version, the .NET ecosystem evolves; NuGet packages, shared DLLs, and popular frameworks are updated; and certain patterns and APIs change or become obsolete. This section guides you through ensuring third-party compatibility, upgrading data access technologies like Entity Framework Core and Dapper, and understanding recent updates in globalization, serialization, and cryptography.

Ensuring Third-Party Compatibility (NuGet, DLLs)

Moving to .NET 10 means you want all your dependencies to be compatible with the new runtime. Start by reviewing every NuGet package referenced in your project. Most active packages publish updates for new .NET versions soon after release, but you could find some that remain outdated or unmaintained. Use the NuGet package manager in Visual Studio or the `dotnet list package --outdated` command to check for updates.

It's important to read release notes for each major library and make sure the versions you're using officially support .NET 10. For rare or custom DLLs, such as libraries from vendors or internal teams, rebuild them against .NET 10 where possible. If the source code isn't available, check the publisher's support channels. Some very old libraries may not work due to binary or source incompatibilities, especially if they reference APIs removed in recent .NET releases or depend on now-unsupported behaviors.

Watch for changes in licensing, security policies, or new package dependencies introduced by the upgrade. In the case of plugin systems or dynamically loaded DLLs, test each plugin in isolation before deploying the whole solution.

Upgrading Data Access Patterns (EF Core, Dapper)

Data access libraries keep evolving with .NET. Entity Framework Core (EF Core) is now the main object-relational mapper (ORM) supported by Microsoft, and with .NET 10, it gains extra performance boosts and expanded features. As you migrate, update your EF Core packages to the latest major version that targets .NET 10; older versions may not be compatible or may not take advantage of new features like improved LINQ translation and optimized database provider support.

If you use Dapper or other micro-ORMs, upgrade these packages as well and test your queries thoroughly. Some API changes, such as adjustments to parameter binding or supported data types, may surface. Review your data models and query logic. New framework versions can have differences in how queries are executed, especially with advanced features like asynchronous streaming or bulk operations.

Check if your database providers (for SQL Server, SQLite, PostgreSQL, etc.) have published compatible driver updates. Database providers sometimes lag a bit behind the main .NET release and may require extra configuration steps or manual updates.

Globalization, Serialization, and Cryptography Updates

.NET 10 continues to refine globalization and localization support. This includes more comprehensive Unicode handling, consistent culture-sensitive operations across platforms, and updates to resource management for applications targeting multiple languages. If your app uses custom globalization logic, like parsing numbers or dates, review any new behaviors specific to your region or language settings.

Serialization has also improved, especially in the `System.Text.Json` library, which now supports more complex types and gives better performance for reading and writing JSON. If your app depends on specific serialization features, like custom converters or compatibility with legacy systems, double-check that your serialization logic still works the same way in .NET 10. For apps using XML or binary serialization, review the documentation for any breaking changes or new security restrictions.

On the cryptography front, .NET 10 strengthens default security settings and introduces additional algorithms and hash functions. Support for outdated or vulnerable protocols (such as some TLS versions) may be removed or disabled by default. If your app interacts with certificates, encryption, or secure protocols, update your usage to rely on recommended .NET 10 approaches and always choose libraries that are regularly updated and audited.

Keeping your libraries and integrations up to date not only ensures a successful .NET 10 migration but also brings improvements in performance, security, and maintainability for your apps.

Containers and Cloud Readiness

Building and running your applications in containers is now a core skill for modern .NET development. .NET 10 makes it even easier to package, deploy, and test your apps in Docker and cloud environments like Kubernetes. This section covers what you should know as you upgrade your project for cloud-readiness and container adoption.

Changes in Default Images and Container Support

.NET 10 brings updated default container images. The official .NET images on Docker Hub now support the latest base operating systems and come with improved security and size optimizations. That means when you write your Dockerfile for a .NET 10 app, you'll use the most up-to-date images, like `mcr.microsoft.com/dotnet/aspnet:10.0` for web apps or `mcr.microsoft.com/dotnet/runtime:10.0` for console apps.

New images often feature reduced attack surfaces by including only what's strictly necessary to run .NET 10, making your containers both smaller and safer. Support for ARM64 and multi-architecture builds is also better, so you can deploy applications on a wide variety of hardware, from cloud servers to IoT devices. Microsoft updates these images regularly with security patches, and they are tested for the latest Linux distributions as well as Windows containers.

Container tooling in .NET 10 integrates more deeply with Visual Studio and the .NET CLI, letting you build, publish, and even debug containers directly from your IDE or command line, which shortens feedback loops and simplifies troubleshooting.

Cloud-Native Migration (Docker, Kubernetes Integration)

Cloud-native migration means adapting your applications to run and scale in modern environments like Docker containers and Kubernetes clusters. .NET 10 supports this migration by providing:

- Native support for Dockerfile generation and publishing from the `dotnet publish` command. You can generate a Dockerfile automatically or use new templates to fine-tune your container setup.

- Built-in health checks and diagnostic endpoints, which are easily discovered by cloud orchestration tools. With .NET 10, you can add endpoints for health, liveness, and readiness checks, all best practices when running apps in Kubernetes.

- Improved configuration and secret management, with tight integration to environment variables and external configuration sources. This aligns with the 12-factor app principles for cloud deployment.

- Support for Kubernetes manifests and Helm chart templates, making it easier to deploy, roll back, and update applications automatically.

When migrating, review your use of environment variables and networking, forecast where your service might need to talk to other containers or cloud services, and test those points with containerized builds. If you're using platform services (like Azure App Services, AWS ECS, or Google Cloud Run), make sure your image builds to the required standards.

Deploying and Testing .NET 10 in Containers

Deploying your .NET 10 application in a container starts with writing a Dockerfile. With .NET 10, the process is simple. You define your build and runtime environment, copy your output files, and set up environment variables for things like connection strings and app settings.

Here's a high-level workflow:

1. Write or generate a Dockerfile in your project. Use the .NET 10 base images.

2. Build the container using `docker build -t myapp:10.0 .` from your project directory.

3. Run the container locally to check that everything starts and responds as expected: `docker run -d -p 8080:80 myapp:10.0`.

4. Test service endpoints, database connections, and external integrations inside the container.

5. Push your image to a container registry (like Docker Hub, Azure Container Registry, or AWS ECR).

6. Deploy to your cloud platform, either directly (for simple Docker hosting) or via Kubernetes manifests and Helm charts for larger systems.

Testing is crucial, and continuous integration (CI) tools like GitHub Actions or Azure DevOps can automate building and running your containers for each commit or pull request. Use these tools to validate each new code or configuration change in a safe, containerized environment before deploying to production.

Finally, keep your images up to date by regularly rebuilding against the latest .NET 10 container base images for security and performance.

Testing, Validation, and Quality Assurance

When migrating to .NET 10, thoroughly testing your applications is one of the most important steps you can take. Proper validation helps you catch issues early, ensure all features still work, and confirm that your application takes advantage of new platform improvements. This section explains core concepts and practices for side-by-side testing, using code quality tools like profilers and linters, and performance profiling in the .NET 10 environment.

Side-by-Side Testing and Functional Verification

Side-by-side testing means running your application on the previous version and .NET 10 simultaneously. By comparing outcomes for typical scenarios, like executing APIs, displaying key screens, or running automated tests, you can quickly spot differences in behavior. This helps uncover subtle issues that static analysis might miss, such as changes in data formatting, error handling, or performance.

To get started, first ensure your old and new environments are set up cleanly. Run your test suites against both versions, paying attention to any failed assertions or differences in results. For web or API projects, send the same HTTP requests to both and compare the responses. For UI apps, visually inspect major workflows in both environments.

Functional verification refers to checking if your core business logic and features work after migration. It involves more than unit testing—user stories, end-to-end scenarios, and integration points all need to be verified. If possible, automate these tests using frameworks like xUnit, NUnit, or MSTest for code, and Playwright or Selenium for UI.

Using Profilers, Linters, and Compatibility Analyzers

Quality tools are essential to finding hidden issues and maintaining high standards in your codebase.

A profiler lets you monitor how your application uses resources such as CPU, memory, and threads. The built-in Visual Studio Diagnostic Tools, `dotnet-trace`, and `dotnet-counters` are all available in .NET 10. Profiler tools can identify memory leaks, inefficient code paths, and unnecessary allocations that might not have been noticeable before the upgrade.

A linter helps maintain code quality by checking for style, errors, and potential bugs according to established coding rules. For .NET, tools like Roslyn analyzers, StyleCop, and third-party linters can scan your projects and surface issues. They're especially useful after migration to .NET 10, as you may have new language features and updated best practices to follow.

For compatibility, the .NET Upgrade Assistant offers built-in analyzers that highlight breaking changes and obsolete APIs. The API Portability Analyzer checks your assemblies against the target platforms to catch APIs that might be missing or behave differently in .NET 10. Running these analyzers as part of your build or CI process catches problems before they reach production.

Performance Profiling Tools in .NET 10

Once functionality and quality checks are complete, focus on performance. .NET 10 includes improvements in startup times, memory usage, and runtime efficiency, but only thorough profiling will show how your specific application behaves.

- Visual Studio Performance Profiler provides real-time insights into CPU, memory, and thread usage, with flame charts and time analysis to pinpoint bottlenecks.

- Dotnet CLI tools such as `dotnet-monitor`, `dotnet-counters`, and `dotnet-dump` offer deep diagnostics from the command line. These are useful for local development and cloud-deployed apps.

- BenchmarkDotNet is a dedicated benchmarking library for micro-performance tests. Integrate it to measure differences between code paths, especially after replacing older APIs during migration.

Regularly running these profilers before and after migration reveals unintentional slowdowns or resource spikes. Use profiling output to make targeted optimizations and validate that the migration resulted in equal, or, ideally, better, performance.

By combining thorough side-by-side testing, code quality checks, and robust performance profiling, you can ensure your .NET 10 migration is secure, stable, and successful, ready for users and future improvements alike.

Pitfalls, Troubleshooting, and Best Practices

Moving your applications to .NET 10 is a significant step forward, but it's not always smooth sailing. It's easy to hit unexpected roadblocks, especially if your codebase spans several years or relies on lots of outside libraries. This section looks at some of the most common issues you might face, ways to spot and fix compatibility problems, strategies for rolling back if things go sideways, and how to keep your DevOps processes running without surprises.

Common Migration Pitfalls

When you start migrating, the first thing you're likely to run into is dependency troubles. Some NuGet packages or custom DLLs you depend on might not yet support .NET 10. Sometimes, these libraries are no longer actively maintained, which means you'll have to search for alternatives or build solutions yourself. It's also easy to overlook APIs that Microsoft no longer supports—things like Web Forms or certain deep reflection features simply don't exist anymore—and this can break builds or cause runtime errors as soon as you try to run your project.

Another pitfall is ignoring the compiler's warnings about outdated or deprecated APIs. These warnings might seem harmless at first, but as obsolete APIs are removed in .NET 10, they quickly become build errors. Similarly, small changes in configuration files, resource handling, or environment variable management, particularly in cloud or containerized environments, can break things unexpectedly, sometimes only showing up after deployment.

How to Diagnose and Fix Compatibility Issues

The key to a smooth migration is catching problems early. If you notice something isn't working, start with the tools that Microsoft provides. Compatibility analyzers like the API Portability Analyzer and the .NET Upgrade Assistant are built to flag known issues as you upgrade. Always check your build output for warnings and errors after migration. Don't assume that just because the app compiles, it's ready for production.

It's a good idea to run your automated tests and compare results between the older and the new version of your application. If you notice failures, look for common patterns: is a particular library or feature at fault? Check the official documentation for .NET 10 breaking changes, as these documents often have code examples and suggested fixes.

For third-party dependencies, visit their documentation or support forums to confirm .NET 10 support. Sometimes, simply updating to the latest version of a library is enough to resolve the issue, but other times you may need to refactor your code to work with a different API set or new patterns introduced in the latest release.

Rollback and Contingency Strategies

It's always nice when a migration goes perfectly, but sometimes things go off the rails. Having a rollback plan is essential. Start by keeping clean backups of your pre-migration projects. Using source control systems like Git makes this easy; you can create a branch or tag before you make any major changes. If your project is large, consider an incremental approach, migrating one component at a time and testing at each stage. That way, if you do run into trouble, only a small part of your app is affected, and you can easily undo just those changes without losing all your progress.

In more advanced setups, deploy both the old and new versions side by side in a staging environment. This approach gives you the flexibility to switch back quickly if needed. For production deployments, automated scripts and infrastructure tools (sometimes called "infrastructure as code") make it possible to roll back a failed deployment at the click of a button. Always document the changes you make during migration; these notes will be invaluable if you need to reverse or debug your adjustments later.

Keeping DevOps Pipelines Compatible

Once your code is ready, your continuous integration and deployment (CI/CD) pipelines need a little attention too. Make sure your build agents are using the .NET 10 SDK, older agents sometimes default to previous versions, leading to mysterious failures that are hard to diagnose. Scrub your build scripts for hardcoded framework versions and get rid of any MSBuild parameters that don't apply with the new SDK-style projects.

Test your end-to-end pipeline, running builds, tests, and deployments as you would for a production release. For shared libraries in your organization, consider using multitargeting to support both .NET 10 and any older consumers who aren't quite ready to upgrade yet.

Performance and error monitoring should be built into your pipeline, so you'll catch slowdowns or test failures early. Keeping these checks in place helps you spot problems quickly and adjust before they impact your users.

By anticipating common pitfalls, learning to diagnose compatibility issues, preparing rollback strategies, and tuning your DevOps pipelines, you'll make your .NET 10 migration not only possible but genuinely rewarding, for you and your development team.

Conclusion and Next Steps

Reaching the end of your migration journey to .NET 10 is an achievement worth celebrating. While the process can feel daunting at times, taking it one step at a time and staying focused on clear, practical goals makes all the difference. Let's wrap up with a look at how to keep your skills and your projects current, the best ways to continue learning, and some encouragement to help you face any future updates with confidence.

Staying Up to Date with .NET Releases

.NET is always evolving, and Microsoft continues to release updates that bring important features, performance boosts, and security fixes. Staying current is not about chasing every new version on the day it comes out, but building habits that make upgrading smoother and less stressful. The .NET team publishes an official release calendar, along with clear LTS windows, so you can plan ahead and avoid unpleasant surprises.

One of the simplest habits is to turn on notifications or subscribe to release blogs and announcements. By following the official .NET blog or the Microsoft Docs update feed, you'll know when new features are on the horizon or when a support period is ending. It's also a good practice to set aside time every few months to review your dependencies, run your projects on the latest preview SDK in a safe environment, and note any warnings or issues that might need attention before the next big upgrade.

Whenever possible, automate your update checks using CI pipelines or DevOps scripts that flag outdated packages or unsupported framework versions. This proactive approach saves time, reduces urgent "fire drills," and makes it easier to incorporate new platform benefits with less effort.

Continuing Education and Resources for .NET 10 Migrators

There has never been a better time to learn about .NET. The online ecosystem is rich with tutorials, video courses, free documentation, and vibrant community forums. Microsoft's own documentation is incredibly comprehensive, with migration guides, code samples, and best practices for every platform and scenario. Bookmark the official .NET Documentation site and use the tutorial sections, which often walk you through real-world scenarios similar to what you'll encounter in your projects.

If you prefer learning by watching, platforms like YouTube offer official .NET community standups, demo sessions, and in-depth guides from both Microsoft engineers and independent experts. There are also coding bootcamps and user groups around the world that focus on .NET, providing plenty of ways to ask questions, share experiences, and learn from others.

Don't overlook the value of community-driven learning, too. Stack Overflow, GitHub repositories, and tech blogs are home to practical migration stories, clever workarounds, and valuable project templates you can adapt for your own use. As .NET 10 matures, more resources and sample projects will appear. Stay curious and explore what others are building.

Encouragement for a Smooth Transition

Every migration comes with its bumps and learning curves, but you've already proven your adaptability by exploring .NET 10. Remember, you aren't alone. Millions of developers worldwide are walking a similar path, learning, stumbling, and sharing solutions every day.

Take pride in the progress you've made, no matter how gradual. Migrating to .NET 10 is not just about following the latest trends but about building a more secure, faster, and future-ready foundation for your work. Embrace challenges as learning opportunities and don't hesitate to ask for help when needed—the .NET community is welcoming and supportive.

Keeping your skills fresh, your tools up to date, and your code ready for the future will serve you well, not just for .NET 10 but for every project ahead.

CHAPTER 10

The Future of .NET

Introduction: The Significance of .NET's Future

The software development industry is a dynamic field. New tools, methods of operation, and innovative concepts are introduced annually. .NET has demonstrated its ability to adapt and develop with the times in this rapidly evolving field. Although it began by assisting developers in creating Windows applications, .NET has evolved into much more. It is compatible with Windows, Linux, macOS, mobile devices, websites, cloud computing, and network edge devices.

Why is this continuous evolution important? Because millions of developers use .NET to solve practical issues. As .NET expands, it simplifies life for groups of all sizes, from big businesses to novice programmers working alone. Updates are included with every new version to make apps safer, faster, and more dependable.

Since they indicate the direction that .NET is taking, this chapter takes a look back at some of the most significant advancements in recent versions:

- **Better performance, more robust cross-platform app support, and significant progress on cloud-native features were all brought about by .NET 8.** The new native AOT (Ahead-of-Time) compilation reduced application size and accelerated app startup. Developers could create genuinely modern apps for any device with the help of tools like Blazor and.NET MAUI.

- **.NET 9 advanced security, web APIs, and more intelligent developer tools.** With more "minimal" code, it made APIs simpler to write and maintain. Language advancements continued to expand on C#'s strength and versatility, while support for containers and cloud computing became even easier.

These trends are carried forward by .NET 10. It is now more unified than ever before, which makes it simpler to use the appropriate tools, whether you are developing for desktop, cloud, mobile, or the web. You will discover the most recent language updates, deeper AI/ML integration, more intelligent diagnostics, and even better performance because of runtime enhancements and memory optimizations.

To put it briefly, .NET continues to grow because our industry does. Every innovation wave in recent years has focused on giving everyone access to the power of contemporary development rather than just introducing flashy new features. The secret to making the most of .NET in the future is to comprehend this spirit of change as we look to the future.

The Evolving .NET Ecosystem

Unified Platform Vision

Today's .NET concept is straightforward: one framework, all platforms. .NET seeks to be present wherever code must run, be it on Windows, Linux, macOS, mobile devices, the web, smart devices, or the cloud. This objective, which is frequently referred to as *One. NET,* is altering the way programmers approach creating software.

Selecting a platform used to frequently require selecting an entirely different technology stack. While a team developing an iOS or Android app had to learn Swift or Java, another team working on a Windows desktop application might use the .NET Framework. Code could hardly ever be shared, and websites required their own tools. As a result, learning paths became more unclear and projects were more difficult to oversee.

Those lines are disappearing. .NET was created with cross-platform compatibility in mind from the beginning. Whether it's a small script, a mobile app, or a large service running in the cloud, the same tools and languages can be used everywhere. This implies spending more time creating what matters and less time relearning things.

The Function of Blazor, MAUI, and Other Frameworks for .NET

.NET provides essential frameworks that close the gaps between operating systems and devices in order to realize this unified vision.

With a single codebase, developers can create apps that run on Windows, macOS, Android, and iOS thanks to .NET MAUI (*multi-platform app UI*). You create your interface once and make any necessary platform adjustments, and it will function everywhere. Teams can support more users without doing twice as much work thanks to this.

Blazor gives the web access to .NET power. C# and .NET are not limited to JavaScript; they can also be used to create client-side web applications. Blazor allows you to create interactive websites that can also be used as hybrid desktop apps, on the server, or in a browser (thanks to WebAssembly). Because of this flexibility, desktop, cloud, and web applications share the same logic and components.

ASP.NET Core, ML.NET, and more round out the stack, letting you build APIs, work with AI, connect to data, and run anywhere you need to, to Kubernetes in the cloud, IoT boards, or powerful GPU machines.

There is more to the shift to "One.NET" than just platforms. The goal is to make the developer community easier to navigate and more interconnected. Businesses can strive for more than just compatibility. Students' paths are more obvious. Additionally, as new technologies emerge—such as artificial intelligence (AI)—.NET is prepared to embrace them as a single, cohesive ecosystem that can be used to build anything, anywhere.

Community and Open-Source Growth

People have had a significant influence on .NET story, which is not just about technology. Developers, enthusiasts, educators, and large corporations all influence the future direction of .NET. A significant change occurred when Microsoft made .NET open-source and accepted community contributions. All of the sudden, anyone could create new concepts, fix bugs, or recommend features. This transparency not only improved the platform but also increased its applicability to real-world tasks.

How the Community Shapes .NET's Roadmap

Today, community input shapes .NET's future just as much as Microsoft's own intentions. Every new release has numerous community-driven updates. Developers use GitHub, official forums, and even social media conversations to report bugs, suggest enhancements, and impact design. Features that began as open-source pull requests or community requests are frequently featured as headline updates at Microsoft Build or .NET Conf.

Performance improvements, cross-platform fixes, API simplifications, and contemporary language features are just a few of the best features in .NET that result directly from these interactions. Anything that makes sense and is desired by enough people usually makes it into the upcoming release. In addition to being quicker, the method is more democratic and useful for regular developers.

The Importance of Open Standards and Cross-Community Partnerships

Open-source is more than just publicly accessible code. Open standards and cross-community collaborations are key to making .NET genuinely global. These days, Python, JavaScript, cloud platforms like Azure, AWS, and Google Cloud, as well as container systems like Docker, are all frequently integrated with .NET.

The core frameworks incorporate standards such as WebAssembly, HTTP/REST, OpenAPI, and others. This guarantees that .NET applications can communicate with other languages and services without any issues. Additionally, learning .NET prepares developers for a world of technology that extends beyond the Microsoft ecosystem.

.NET becomes more future-proof through collaboration with other open-source projects, whether they are for web user interface, data science, AI, or Kubernetes orchestration. .NET ecosystem develops, adapts, and remains at the forefront by collaborating closely with these communities rather than constantly starting from scratch.

Why This Matters for the Future

This open-standards, community-first methodology has made .NET more flexible than before. Using the best tools for the job, developers can add what is missing, fix what is broken, and vote with their feet. Your input really influences the roadmap, regardless of whether you work as a lone programmer or for a large corporation. .NET is moving toward greater openness, collaboration, and preparedness for whatever the developers of the future may come up with.

Advances in JIT and Native AOT

Just-In-Time (JIT) Compilation Improvements in .NET 8–10

Just-In-Time (JIT) compilation, which dynamically converts IL (*intermediate language*) code to optimized machine code at runtime, is essential to .NET's runtime performance. The JIT has advanced significantly between .NET 8 and .NET 10:

- **Minimization of abstraction penalties:** .NET 10 brought optimizations that reduce the performance cost of using LINQ, enumerables, interfaces, and other abstractions. For example, there are now substantially fewer overheads when using constructs like foreach loops on arrays via interfaces. Compared to direct array iteration, using foreach over an interface array in .NET 9 resulted in a five to six times overhead. This decreases to less than two times in .NET 10, bringing high-level abstractions considerably closer to "bare metal" performance.

- **Smarter code generation:** The JIT has improved its ability to generate efficient code, which has sped up and reduced the resource usage of real-world scenarios like using generics or iterating through arrays. In order to reduce heap allocations and increase cache friendliness, the runtime now more accurately determines when it can stack-allocate small arrays and value types.

- **Improvements to garbage collection (GC):** Region-based reporting, sophisticated memory tuning, and shorter pause times, all of which are critical for web servers and cloud apps, are among the enhancements. The performance of interactive applications has been further improved by write-barrier optimizations that have decreased overall pause durations.

These advancements eliminate the traditional tradeoff of high abstraction causing slowdowns, allowing modern .NET applications to run faster, use less memory, and scale to larger workloads.

Native Ahead-of-Time (AOT) Compilation: Impact on Startup, Memory, and Deployment

Native Ahead-of-Time (AOT) compilation eliminates the need for JIT at runtime by compiling .NET applications completely into native machine code before they are ever executed. Originally released in .NET 8 and rapidly developing in .NET 10, this technology offers a few benefits:

- **Near-instant startup:** Applications, particularly microservices, small web APIs, and command-line tools, can start up nearly instantly by eliminating any runtime compilation. For workloads involving Kubernetes and serverless functions, where new instances spin up continuously, this is invaluable.

- **Low memory footprint:** Native AOT lowers the memory usage of active processes by doing away with the requirement for JIT infrastructure and related metadata at runtime. Because of this, .NET apps can run in resource-constrained environments, like containers and Internet of Things (IoT) devices, and still take advantage of .NET's large API surface.

- **Small deployment sizes:** Only the code that is truly used is packaged in native AOT apps. This trimming reduces the attack surface, streamlines docker image sizes, speeds up downloads, and results in smaller deployments with fewer dependencies.

- **Cross-platform support:** Native AOT enables .NET to extend beyond conventional servers to edge devices and a variety of cloud infrastructures by supporting Windows, Linux, macOS, and ARM architectures.

Practical Impact

Native AOT is perfect for workloads that need little cold start overhead, microservices, and CLI tools. Traditional JIT still offers more flexibility for larger web apps and those that require runtime code generation or reflection, but the AOT toolchain is rapidly expanding to accommodate more scenarios.

Depending on the requirements of the project, developers can select between AOT for maximum efficiency and JIT for maximum flexibility. For AOT publishing, .NET platform offers straightforward tool commands that produce a native binary that is self-contained.

Lower-Level Optimizations in .NET 10

Lower-level runtime and language improvements in .NET 10 have significantly increased raw computational speed and efficiency, which is especially advantageous for workloads requiring memory-sensitive buffering, real-time computation, and intensive data processing. The allocation of stacks is one of the main enhancements. Heap allocation was the primary method used in the past to create temporary buffers or small arrays, which resulted in increased memory and garbage collection overhead. Many of these short-lived or small allocations can now be made efficiently on the stack instead of the heap, thanks to the latest version of .NET. Because stack-allocated structures are automatically discarded when their scope ends, no garbage collection is necessary. This results in faster memory access and instant cleanup. In reality, it is now possible to write more straightforward yet incredibly efficient code for tasks like buffer manipulation, parsing, and iterative computations. Similar to this, array devirtualization enables loops and common access patterns to be converted into faster, hardware-friendly machine code by allowing the runtime to statically determine an array's type, thereby avoiding needless virtual dispatch.

The most recent AVX (*advanced vector extensions*) and SIMD (*single instruction, multiple data*) instructions in .NET 10 have increased support for hardware acceleration in addition to these allocation and abstraction enhancements. The JIT compiler now takes advantage of wide vector registers found in contemporary CPUs like the AVX2 and AVX-512 to vectorize operations on arrays and Span<T>. Transparency and adaptability are used to achieve this: the runtime probes the underlying processor at startup, allowing the use of the fastest and most extensive vector instructions without requiring the developer to modify any code. Numerical operations, data transformations, and intensive algorithms, like those used in statistical computation, image processing, and large-scale analytics, are thus carried out at significantly faster speeds.

These developments have a significant impact on scientific and high-performance computing in .NET, as well as workloads related to AI and machine learning. Libraries for AI and data science can now manipulate tensors, matrixes, and multidimensional datasets with speed and memory efficiency comparable to low-level native code, thanks to new stack allocation semantics and array optimizations. By ensuring that ML.NET's core algorithms and those of compatible libraries run at the full hardware bandwidth, auto-vectorization enables high-throughput, low-latency computation for inferencing, feature extraction, and model scoring. Similarly, .NET 10 runtime now provides the raw capability to manage massive data streams and carry out real-time transformations without the performance snags that were previously connected to managed environments for scientific computing and backend analytics pipelines.

Together, these enhancements establish .NET 10 as a sophisticated, high-performance platform that is actually appropriate for contemporary, computationally demanding workloads. Concise, idiomatic C# can now handle tasks that previously required complex tuning or even the use of unmanaged code, all while automatically utilizing the newest hardware capabilities and enjoying the safety, productivity, and cross-platform universality of .NET.

Memory and Garbage Collection Innovations

Memory management and garbage collection have advanced to a new level of precision and flexibility in .NET 10. The runtime uses a much more intelligent, adaptive garbage collection process that actively examines system conditions and application behavior. This results in shorter pauses and less interference for running applications by enabling the garbage collector to make more informed decisions about when and how thoroughly to clean up memory. For instance, the garbage collector may decide to delay complete collections in order to minimize needless CPU overhead if the system determines that your application has a comparatively low allocation rate. On the other hand, the collector can become more assertive in situations that require a lot of memory or are heavily loaded, making sure that resources are recovered quickly to preserve stability and performance.

The addition of new tuning options and comprehensive diagnostics in .NET 10 is another improvement that gives developers much more control over memory use. Developers can observe and examine garbage collection behavior at a never-before-seen level of detail, thanks to the runtime's exposure of region-based data, such as the size and fragmentation of each memory region. These new diagnostics make it much easier to identify the source of memory pressure and modify garbage collection settings appropriately. Now, developers can modify environment variables, like setting system-level limits to limit memory or changing the region size for the small object heap. Reducing the region size can reduce waste and maintain efficient memory usage for workloads that encounter small working sets and numerous heaps, which is frequently the case in microservice scenarios. On the other hand, expanding the region size can give high-load or throughput-critical services the headroom they need to operate at their best.

Applications can scale more smoothly under real-world load thanks to enhancements made to the garbage collector in .NET 10 that decrease pause times and fragmentation. They have even improved the *write-barrier,* a low-level subsystem that is essential for controlling memory references during collection. In certain microbenchmarks, this update might result in a minor increase in write overhead, but the tradeoff is worthwhile. Because there are significantly fewer and shorter GC pauses in practice, interactive applications, like web servers, background services, and apps running on contemporary ARM64 hardware are generally more responsive and dependable.

In the end, these advancements in memory and garbage collection give programmers more control and better performance. Developers now have the tools to identify, optimize, and resolve memory issues before they become problems, and applications can dynamically adjust to shifting workloads and environments. The end product is a .NET 10 platform that offers unparalleled efficiency and predictability in handling bigger, more complex, and more varied application scenarios.

Security and Reliability in a Changing World
Evolving Authentication, Authorization, and Cryptography

A significant update to its security infrastructure is brought about by .NET 10, which offers a more reliable and smoother authentication and authorization process. Support for OpenID Connect providers and Windows Authentication is comparable, and the integration with Microsoft Entra ID (formerly Azure AD) is now more seamless. The ability to set up distributed token caching and secure API calls much more easily is one of the major innovations.

The platform now enables the registration of named HTTP clients that take care of authentication and token refresh automatically, eliminating the need for developers to manually manage access tokens for APIs. This lessens the possibility of mistakes and vulnerabilities brought about by manual token management and frees developers to concentrate on business logic. Redis, SQL Server, or Azure Cosmos DB have made it easier to set up a dependable, secure token cache for distributed applications that run across multiple servers, ensuring consistent authentication and session continuity at scale.

With support for modern encryption, enhanced data protection APIs, and integration hooks for third-party security providers, the integrated cryptography stack keeps evolving to meet industry standards and new best practices.

Proactive Adaptation to New Security Threats

.NET 10 places a strong emphasis on proactive adaptation and resilience in response to increasingly complex cyberthreats. The extensive disclosure of authentication and authorization metrics is among the most noticeable developments. Metrics for sign-in/sign-out events, authentication challenges and forbids (like unsuccessful login attempts or access denials), and login duration are automatically generated by the framework. Teams can quickly identify spikes in failures, misconfigurations, or potential attacks by using this data to feed into observability tools like Prometheus and Azure Monitor, or command-line dashboards.

By quickly recognizing authentication bottlenecks, configuration mistakes, or anomalies in access patterns, developers and operations can respond to emerging threats or system misconduct before it becomes more serious. Applications are protected by design and actively guarded against new vulnerabilities thanks to this real-time visibility into security operations.

Support for cloud scenarios and containerization is another example of .NET 10's dedication to security. The most recent images are regularly updated with security patches and constructed with smaller attack surfaces. Applications are kept resilient in a shifting threat landscape by the platform's proactive approach, which includes improved diagnostics, update mechanisms, and smooth cryptography upgrades.

Resilient Cloud and Distributed Systems
Built-In Support for Cloud-Native Patterns

With the deeply integrated experience that .NET 10 offers cloud-native developers, developers can easily create, launch, and maintain applications in contemporary distributed environments. .NET 10 comes with built-in support for containerization, which allows apps to be packaged as more compact and secure Docker images than ever before. These images are made to only contain the components required for the application to function, which lowers vulnerabilities and enhances cold-start efficiency. To keep deployments safe and compliant, the platform frequently applies the most recent security patches to these base images.

The improved multi-architecture support of .NET 10 enables smooth deployment to ARM64-based infrastructure, IoT devices, and a broad range of Linux or Windows server environments in addition to the conventional x64 targets. Applications can operate reliably on cloud, edge, and cross-platform environments thanks to this flexibility. Development for distributed systems is made even easier by the integration with .NET Aspire. By standardizing telemetry and health checks, automating service discovery, and setting up secure connections, Aspire manages intricate orchestration requirements. Aspire makes it easier to scale distributed solutions and facilitates more seamless cloud migrations by making the process of connecting frontend, backend, and supporting microservices more dependable and repeatable.

High Availability, Failover, and Telemetry Advances

.NET 10 offers notable enhancements for high availability and observability in recognition of the crucial requirements of fault tolerance and reliability in the current cloud environment. Deployment patterns are optimized for seamless web farm or cluster operation, multi-node failover, and rolling updates. Even when services scale horizontally or move across datacenters, persistent, secure authentication is supported by easier-to-configure distributed token caches and data protection across nodes.

With native OpenTelemetry support that allows for distributed tracing, metrics collection, and logging with virtually no setup, telemetry has become a top priority. Dashboards like Prometheus, Azure Monitor, or Aspire's built-in tools provide developers with instant access to insights on user activity, application performance, and health. This degree of real-time observability guarantees that problems can be identified early, addressed promptly, and thoroughly examined after the fact.

Additionally, ASP.NET Core and .NET Aspire offer native integration with orchestrators such as Kubernetes through automated health checks, readiness, and liveness probes. In order to preserve overall application availability and minimize interruption for end users, a single service or node that becomes unhealthy is automatically isolated and recycled. Changes in the cloud environment (like scaling events or service restarts) have little effect on operations and do not require developer intervention because configuration management and service endpoint discovery are centrally managed.

With these improvements, .NET 10 positions itself as a stable, future-ready platform for resilient distributed systems, making it easier for teams implementing contemporary cloud-native and DevOps techniques and guaranteeing that comprehensive telemetry, failover, and high availability are always accessible.

Modern Application Development Toolkit
API Design and Minimalism

The foundation of today's web development in .NET 10 is minimal APIs. By concentrating on the fundamentals of function-first API surface, they provide a simplified method of defining HTTP endpoints with only a few lines of code. This method promotes a more readable and maintainable codebase in addition to reducing boilerplate code. Without the fuss and intricacy typically associated with MVC patterns, developers can quickly set up routes, bind parameters, and connect to data stores or services using minimal APIs. Developers use short lambda expressions or local functions that explicitly define the purpose of each operation rather than inheriting from big controller classes or setting up complex routing.

The evolution of API design has shifted significantly in favor of developer usability and simplification with .NET 10. Making routine development tasks as easy as possible is the guiding idea. Smarter defaults like automatic model validation, integrated OpenAPI (Swagger) documentation, top-level statements for quick startup, and smooth dependency injection support are examples of usability. Furthermore, .NET 10 allows developers to combine traditional controller-based patterns with minimal APIs in a single application, allowing them to use full-featured MVC when more complexity is needed and a minimalist approach when it is appropriate.

Rapid prototyping, microservices development, and the creation of cloud-ready HTTP services are now all possible by the dedication to simplicity and clarity. The simplicity of the daily developer experience is further reinforced by features like validation based on data annotations, enhanced error feedback, and syntax highlighting for route templates. .NET 10 guarantees that API design is no longer a barrier but rather a driving force behind the creation of contemporary applications by emphasizing clear, understandable patterns that scale from basic prototypes to production systems.

Cross-Platform User Experience
The Evolution of .NET MAUI

The foundation of cross-platform user interface development in the .NET ecosystem is now .NET MAUI (multi-platform app UI). .NET MAUI, which was first developed from Xamarin. Forms, enables you to create a single codebase that functions natively on Windows, macOS, Android, and iOS. By enhancing the developer experience, enhancing app performance, and updating interface design, MAUI in .NET 10 promotes quality and productivity.

In order to significantly reduce boilerplate code and speed up UI development, the framework now supports streamlined XAML with global and implicit XML namespaces. Namespaces need to be specified only once by developers, keeping files neat and consistent. Older components like `ListView` and `TableView` are replaced by controls like `CollectionView` and `CarouselView`, which offer improved data virtualization, flexible layouts, and smoother rendering. Async patterns have been incorporated into animation APIs, enabling responsive, choreographed transitions using straightforward `await` logic.

Through simple integration with .NET Aspire, MAUI also adds new features that automate difficult tasks like advanced telemetry, service discovery, and configuration management. Platform-specific improvements also guarantee that every app feels native, including updated accessibility APIs to comply with the most recent Apple standards, new popover handling for modals on iOS and Mac, full support for Android API 36 and JDK 21, and text input controls that feel native on all platforms. By doing this, developers can reach a wider audience and guarantee a consistent, modern experience across desktop and mobile platforms.

Significant advancements have been made in memory usage, rendering, and app startup, giving users faster launches and more seamless interactions. A UI toolkit that facilitates scalable, high-quality apps for almost any device is the end result, which lowers friction and frees up developers' time to concentrate on the user experience.

Blazor Advancements for Device-Consistent UIs

Blazor in .NET 10 makes it possible to create genuinely cross-device user experiences for desktop, web, and hybrid applications. Blazor enables C# and .NET developers to create dynamic, rich user interfaces that can be used on the server, in the browser (using WebAssembly), or as hybrid desktop/mobile apps. By utilizing Blazor components in MAUI, the hybrid model allows you to reuse UI elements and business logic across all these environments.

.NET 10 prioritizes developer performance and usability. Users experience significantly smaller downloads and instant caching when Blazor scripts are served as static assets. Whether apps are desktop hybrids or run on the web, the diagnostics tooling is more comprehensive and provides developers with comprehensive information about memory and performance. The advent of dynamic UI features—like QuickGrid's dynamic row styling, enhanced modal and reconnection experiences, and flexible navigation—makes it possible to create polished, adaptable interfaces that feel seamless wherever users interact.

Blazor's declarative state persistence ensures that the state is maintained during interactive and prerendered sessions, which is necessary for seamless device transitions and offline functionality. Building secure enterprise-class apps that function consistently across desktop, mobile, and web form factors is made simpler by improved authentication and security infrastructure. Native support for Server-Sent Events (SSE) ups the ante on interaction by facilitating real-time updates and monitoring, which is essential for dashboards, notifications, and teamwork tools.

Blazor is now a top-tier platform for creating genuinely device-consistent, scalable user interfaces with contemporary development patterns, thanks to these platform enhancements, robust code reuse, and a thriving component ecosystem.

Enhancements in Tooling and Productivity

Smarter CLI

The .NET 10 version of the command-line interface (CLI) is even more convenient and user-friendly. One of the main improvements is that, in the majority of use cases, developers no longer need to manually specify the `--interactive` option for interactive terminal sessions. Tasks like retrieving NuGet credentials and interacting with commands that prompt the user are more user-friendly as a result. This simplification will be expanded upon in later releases with additional interactive CLI features like progress bars and integrated prompting.

IDE Experience: Visual Studio, VS Code, and Rider

AI-powered IntelliCode in Visual Studio boosts productivity by predicting and suggesting code completions that developers are most likely to use using machine learning models trained on massive codebases. IntelliCode prioritizes context-appropriate methods and property suggestions while highlighting likely code completions. Since refactoring tools have been upgraded for .NET 10, simple transformations (such as changing variables throughout a solution or converting loops to LINQ) are now only a click away. These changes are frequently indicated by an obvious lightbulb indicator in the editor.

With AI integration through GitHub Copilot, Visual Studio Code (VS Code) continues to be a top cross-platform editor for .NET. With the use of comments and code logic, Copilot can anticipate, produce, and add to your code, offering context-aware suggestions or even creating documentation and tests. Integrated AI tools that can automatically produce snippets, enhance code organization, and recommend test scaffolds or documentation are especially helpful to developers using ReSharper or JetBrains Rider.

Testing Workflows

With native support for the Microsoft Testing Platform made possible by the improved `dotnet test` command, testing in .NET 10 is more reliable. Teams can benefit from consistent test discovery, execution, and reporting across various project types by including the new test runner in the configuration. Because the platform is extensible, new test adapters and runners can be easily integrated, making it simpler to update and implement testing standards.

Code Analysis and Refactoring

.NET developers are now accustomed to doing deeper, more intelligent code analysis on a daily basis. By using advanced strategies like late devirtualization and method inlining, the JIT compiler in .NET 10 removes performance snags during array and collection processing. Because of these developments, refactoring is safer because developers are less likely to experience performance regressions when switching between different types of loops or collections. Additionally, these runtime optimizations are combined with static analysis in IDEs to provide insightful warnings or recommendations throughout the development process, improving code quality and safety.

AI-Assisted Development

The .NET development process is now closely linked to AI assistants like JetBrains AI, GitHub Copilot, and Visual Studio IntelliCode. From code creation and completion to automatic documentation and even pull request review recommendations, these tools assist in automating a wide range of tasks. Leading AI development tools have the following features:

- Using context and natural language comments to forecast entire code blocks and functions.

- Suggesting clever refactorings to adhere to best standards, including simplifying methods, switching imperative code to LINQ, or dividing classes.

- Creating automated tests and making recommendations for ways to increase test coverage.

- Supplying interactive, chatbot-style Q&A for troubleshooting tips or API/SDK documentation within the editor.

- Using AI-powered PR feedback and commit message auto-complete to speed up code review.

Multiple IDEs and editors can be used with AI features, and they are starting to enable other workflows, including hands-free operation, local execution for speed and privacy, and voice or gesture-based coding.

What You Can Expect Beyond .NET 10

The Microsoft ecosystem is talking more and more about "what is next" as .NET 10 develops and establishes itself as a cohesive, cross-platform development platform. A number of indicators suggest potential future paths that could shape .NET's development in the upcoming years, guided by Microsoft's open roadmaps, emerging technological trends, and expanding community influence.

Agility and modularity are currently the cornerstones of Microsoft's approach, and this will probably continue. To reduce breaking changes and facilitate version migration, regular, fast releases will continue to be made, combining Long-Term Support (LTS) with feature-driven interim versions. Migrations have already become more predictable, thanks to tools like .NET Upgrade Assistant and API Portability Analyzer, which are being improved with better diagnostics to identify game-changing changes early. This strategy helps developers stay up to date with little difficulty while also boosting confidence for commercial projects.

As demonstrated by .NET Aspire and advancements in containerization, cloud-native and distributed application readiness is poised to gain even more prominence. In addition to substantially reducing container image sizes and attack surfaces, efforts are being made to increase support for several architectures, including ARM64 and emerging hardware platforms. Strong priority will remain on security and smooth cloud interaction, from Azure to third-party platforms. The industry-wide shift toward microservices, observability, and scalable app deployment is reflected in these advancements.

Both as features and underlying runtime improvements, AI and machine learning will become increasingly popular. Future iterations are anticipated to bring AI workloads even closer to the core .NET runtime following the integration of native AI APIs in .NET 9. This might entail deeper hooks into cloud AI services, tighter ML .NET integration, and more smooth GPU offloading, all while maintaining friendly developer onboarding and easily available learning materials.

Anticipate a greater emphasis on ubiquitous cross-platform user experience, powered by frameworks like Blazor and .NET MAUI. In addition to achieving compatibility among Windows, Linux, macOS, iOS, and Android, there is a drive to reveal a single user interface toolkit and further integrate device capabilities. Intelligent IDE extensions are directing design and the shift to these more adaptable paradigms, and the community is already witnessing controls, layouts, and animation models that change during runtime.

Participation in the open-source community will continue to be essential. The out-of-the-box developer experience is increasingly shaped by third-party libraries, controls, and diagnostic extensions, and Microsoft still welcomes community feedback through GitHub. More open RFCs, direct voting on feature proposals, and greater openness regarding breaking changes or deprecations are all things to anticipate.

Lastly, accessibility and performance are top concerns. It is expected that JIT compilation and garbage collection performance gains will quicken, especially as .NET expands into serverless, cloud, and IoT applications. As standards grow and feedback from a wide range of international developers is included into each release cycle, accessibility and internationalization will progress.

To put it briefly, .NET platform is advancing toward intelligent, cloud-connected, and device-agnostic development while preparing for a future characterized by dependability, security, speed, and openness. With forward and backward compatibility as a driving concept, developers can expect quick advancements, making the adoption of new versions safer and more seamless than before.

Conclusion: Preparing for the Future with .NET

One thing is evident as you get to the end of this journey through .NET 10 and beyond: the .NET ecosystem is more dynamic, aspirational, and welcoming than it has ever been. The road ahead is full of innovation and growth prospects, whether you are developing your first app or managing a multi-decade legacy system.

The best recommendation for students is to embrace .NET's modular and dynamic nature. Concentrate on grasping the following fundamentals: solid object-oriented ideas, proficiency with contemporary C#, and familiarity with both desktop and cloud concepts. Start small, try new features like AI-driven code recommendations and file-based apps, and always rely on the robust community resources like official documentation, forums, and open-source repositories. Do not be scared to break things; practical experimentation and adaptability will shape your best abilities.

Now is the ideal moment for seasoned professionals to review best practices and get teams ready for continuous change. Encourage an engineering culture that encourages pragmatic refactoring and honors ongoing learning. To maintain your solution current and safe, take the time to automate testing and migration processes. To ensure that everyone on your team takes advantage of what is possible with the .NET of today and tomorrow, promote knowledge exchange regarding cutting-edge technologies like cloud-native application paradigms, containerization, and AI-assisted development.

Develop curiosity and adaptability to survive and prosper as the tale of .NET unfolds. Accept Microsoft's new innovation rhythm; use every release as an opportunity to streamline your stack, pay off technical debt, or open completely new application scenarios. Make performance, accessibility, and cross-platform reach your top priorities to ensure that your work is inclusive to a worldwide audience and future-proof.

Above all, keep in mind that the people of .NET are its greatest asset. Developers advance the platform through innovative applications, insightful criticism, and a strong sense of community. The next chapter is shaped by your contributions, your efforts, and your openness to learning.

Let your own .NET adventure be open-ended when this book draws to an end; it should be characterized by curiosity, resiliency, and the self-assurance to create whatever comes next. With .NET, here's to your future: motivated by the present, prepared for the future, and constantly willing to create.

Index

A

Abstraction penalty, 138–139, 141

Advanced Vector Extensions 10.2 (AVX10.2), 153, 154

Ahead-of-Time (AOT), 207, 212

AI, *see* Artificial intelligence (AI)

Android

    API 36 and JDK 21, 117

    editor and entry controls, 118, 119

    webview fullscreen video playback, 117, 118

Animation API modernization

    async animation methods, 113

    practical usage and migration, 113, 114

AOT, *see* Ahead-of-Time (AOT)

API Portability Analyzer, 183, 186, 201, 203, 223

AppCompatEditText, 118

Apple M-series, 147

Application architecture, 40, 188

Arm64 chips, 148

Array to ReadOnlySpan, 30

Array to Span, 30

Artificial intelligence (AI), 154, 208–210, 213, 222

ASP.NET Core and Blazor, 5, 8

ASP.NET Web API, 37

Async animation methods, 113, 114

Auth0, 86

Authentication, 39, 54–57, 83, 84, 86, 93, 119, 122, 129, 194, 215–217, 220

Automatic validation, 52

Auto-property syntax, 22

AVX10.2, *see* Advanced Vector Extensions 10.2 (AVX10.2)

B

Behavioral change, 188

BenchmarkDotNet, 202

Benchmarks, 142, 144, 148

Binary incompatibility, 187

Blazor, 59, 66, 75, 79, 88–93, 184, 194, 209, 219, 220, 223

    community, 60

    JavaScript file, 62

    MSBuild properties, 63

    NavLink component, 81

    .NET 10, 60, 63

    .NET ecosystem, 60

    objective, 71

    path, 61

    role, 60

    runtime diagnostics, 63

    script, 62

    script file, 62

    templates, 72

    versions, 76, 80

    WebAssembly technology, 60

Boilerplate code, 12, 19, 22, 38, 40–42, 75, 76, 79, 88, 99, 100, 161, 162, 171, 193, 218, 219

Buffer manipulation, 30, 213

Building secure web apps, 83

C

C#
    advantages, 14
    async and await, 11
    C# 2.0, 11
    C# 3.0, 11
    C# 5.0, 11
    C# 6.0 and 7.x, 12
    C# 8.0, 12
    C# 14, 12, 19–34
    development experience, 14
    file-based C# apps, 13
    file-level directives, 15–17
    scripting languages, 15
    sharing, 14
    shebang (#!), 18, 19
    simplicity and flexibility, 14
    virtual project in memory, 15
C# 14, 12, 13
    caller data, 27
    constructors, 32, 33
    extension members, 19–21, 35
    features, 4
    field keyword, 21–23
    lambda parameter modifiers, 26, 27
    log metrics, 28
    nameof operator, 24–26, 35
    null-conditional assignment, 23, 24, 35
    parse a configuration value, 28
    partial event, 33, 34
    ref readonly parameter, 28
    Span<int>, 29
    Span<T> and
        ReadOnlySpan<T>, 29–31
    target delegate/method signature, 27
    unbound generic types, 24–26, 35
CarouselView, 104, 107, 110, 128, 219

CI/CD, *see* Continuous integration and
        deployment (CI/CD)
CLI, *see* Command-line interface (CLI)
CloseColumnOptionsAsync, 68
Cloud-native migration, 198
CLR, *see* Common Language
        Runtime (CLR)
CollectionView, 104–106, 110–112, 128,
        129, 219
ColorPicker, 109, 128
Common Language Runtime (CLR), 7
Command-line interface (CLI), 16, 98,
        192, 198, 202, 212, 220
Community-driven learning, 205
Community-first methodology, 210
Compatibility, 203
    analyzers, 201, 203
    binary, 187
    importance, 182
    and migration, 182
    source, 187–188
    third-party, 196
Constructors, 32
    declare, 32, 33
    partial, 32, 33
Contemporary web development, 189
Content Security Policy (CSP), 74
Continuous integration and deployment
        (CI/CD) pipelines, 204
Continuous integration (CI) tools, 200
Control enhancements
    CarouselView, 107
    CollectionView, 104–106
    deprecated controls and
        migration, 109–112
    entry and editor controls, 107, 108
    HybridWebView, 108
    SearchBar and Switch, 108, 109

Controller-based APIs, 37–39, 41,
43, 48, 50
Cryptography, 189, 196, 197, 215, 216
CSP, *see* Content Security Policy (CSP)

D

Data access libraries, 196
Data-rich applications, 92
DatePicker, 125, 126
DateTime, 167, 174–176
Declare constructors, 32, 33
Defining declaration, 32
Deployment patterns, 217
Deprecated controls
CarouselView, 110
ImageCell, 110
ListView, 110
and migration strategies, 110–112
SwitchCell, 110
TableView, 110
TextCell, 110
Desktop and mobile developers, 2
Devirtualization, 138, 178, 213, 221
DevOps processes, 202
DevOps techniques, 218
Distributed systems, 179, 216–218
DockLayout, 109, 128
Documentation, 203
dotnet-counters, 54, 56, 149, 150, 152, 156,
201, 202

E

EF Core, *see* Entity Framework Core
(EF Core)
Encrypted token cache, 85
End-user desktop apps, 173

Entity Framework Core (EF Core), 157,
165, 196
admin panel, 167
aggregation patterns, 160
application, 163
Azure Cosmos DB, 163
cloud environments, 172
compiled code, 173
compiled models, 172
Cosmos DB, 164
Cosmos DB integration
improvements, 166
database command, 162
data protection, 169
DateOnly and TimeOnly, 167
DateTime and TimeSpan types, 167
dbcontext optimize command, 173
diagnostics and observability, 179
diagnostics and privacy, 170
ExecuteUpdateAsync, 161–163
ISOWeek class, 174
LeftJoin and RightJoin, 159
libraries, 157, 174
library application, 159
library performance, 177
LINQ expressions, 160
LINQ support and intelligent SQL
generation, 158
manual casting, 168
memory, 161
memory and time, 162
MIN, MAX, and DISTINCT, 169
model configuration, 171
.NET applications, 166
.NET libraries, 157
operations leverage, 169
parameter, 170
patterns, 157, 158

Entity Framework Core (EF Core) (*cont.*)
    query and performance, 169
    SQL commands, 170
    Status and ProcessedAt, 162
    string-related database
        functions, 168
Entry and editor controls, 107, 108, 118
Error monitoring, 204
EventPipe support, 64
JavaScript EventSource API, 88
EXIF metadata, 123
Extension indexers, 19, 20
Extension members, 19–21, 35
Extension methods, 11, 19, 31, 35, 115,
        193, 194
Extension properties, 19, 20, 35

F

FadeToAsync, 113, 114
field keyword, 21–23
File-level directives
    file-based C# apps, 15
    #:package, 16
    #:property, 17
    #:sdk, 16, 17
Direct foreach loops, 141
Functional verification, 200, 201

G

Garbage collection (GC), 144, 147,
        155, 214
    memory usage, 155
    metrics APIs, 155
Garbage collector (GC), 145, 147
GC, *see* Garbage collection (GC); Garbage
    collector (GC)

Generic collection, 7, 178
Geolocation, 119–122
GitHub repository, 4
Globalization and localization, 197
Global XML namespace, 99, 100
GlobalXmlns.cs file, 100

H

HandlePoint, 136
Handling missing, 82
Hot paths, 134, 139
Hybrid search features, 166
HybridWebView, 108

I

IEnumerable, 135, 141, 178, 179
Implementing declaration, 32
Implicit XML namespace,
        99, 100, 219
Integration tests, 40, 41
IntelliCode, 221
Intelligent document
        discovery, 164
iOS and Mac Catalyst
    accessibility, 115, 116
    Apple frameworks, 115
    modal pages, 115
    popovers, 115
IReadOnlyList, 141
IsInAccessibleTree, 115

J

JavaScript, 12, 59, 60, 62, 72, 80, 91, 209
JavaScript console, 64
Just-In-Time (JIT)

compilation, 211
compiler, 139, 213
optimizations, 141

K

Kubernetes, 198–200, 209, 210, 212, 217

L

Lambda expressions, 11, 12, 26, 27, 35, 162, 194, 218
Lambda parameter modifiers, 26, 27, 35
Legacy records, 165
Less memory, 132, 133, 177, 211
LINQ methods, 139
LINQ pipeline, 142
ListView, 104, 109, 110, 112, 128, 219
Living technology, 5
Long-term support (LTS), 183, 222
Loop inversion, 134–136
Lower-level runtime, 213
LTS, *see* Long-term support (LTS)

M

Matrix transformations, 176
MauiAppCompatEditText, 118
MAUI NuGet packages, 97
MAUI workload, 96–98
MediaPicker, 123–125, 129
Memory
    consumption, 189
    dumps, 65
    fragmentation, 146, 147
    management, 148, 214
    usage, 133
Method tiering, 155, 156

Metrics, 54, 55, 149, 156, 216
Microservices development, 218
Microsoft ecosystem, 210, 222
Microsoft Testing Platform, 221
Middleware registration, 194
Migration, 181, 184, 203, 206
    API descriptions, 193
    apps or libraries, 182
    ASP.NET apps, 192
    Blazor, 194
    classification, 187
    compiler's warnings, 202
    full and incremental, 185
    hardware and OS, 184
    library, 183
    LTS, 183
    middleware, 194
    .NET 10, 186
    .NET MAUI application, 195
    NuGet's dependency, 183
    performance, 185
    platform features, 195
    project layouts, 183
    risks, 185
    routing, 194
    security and logins, 194
    tools, 186
    UI projects, 195
    web APIs, 193
Minimal APIs, 38, 50
    controller-based APIs, 38
    enable validation, 50
    .NET 10, 53
    validation, 50
Model configuration, 171
Modern API-driven applications, 54
Modernization, 41
Modernization process, 190

Modifiers, 12, 26–29, 35
Monolithic apps, 190

N

nameof operator, 24–26, 35
Navigation, 79, 82, 90–93, 115, 116, 127,
194, 220
.NET
adventure, 225
capabilities, 9
Core, 133
developer, 3
development, 2, 3, 155
ecosystem, 1, 8, 9, 196, 210, 219
history, 7
.NET Framework 1.0., 7
.NET framework to .NET 10, 8, 189
platform, 224
team, 204
telemetry, 180
Upgrade Assistant, 201
versions, 8, 48
.NET 5, 8
.NET 6, 8
.NET 7, 8
.NET 8, 8, 83
.NET 9, 8
.NET 10, 38–41, 54, 56, 76, 78, 80, 84–87,
89–93, 132, 137, 180, 192
application, 199
capabilities, 4
concurrency, 151
core infrastructure, 42
environment, 200
features, 3, 39
implementation, 3
migration, 188

.NET MAUI (*see* .NET MAUI)
optimizations, 133
reconnection states and events, 74
SDK, 96
strategic knowledge, 3, 4
.NET Aspire
configuration management, 103
control enhancements, 103–112
NuGet packages, 101
project templates, 102
service discovery, 103
stages of experience, 104
telemetry, 103
templates, 101
tools, 101
.NET MAUI, 8, 9
animation API modernization, 113, 114
DatePicker and TimePicker, 125, 126
developers and users, 95
faster app startup, 127
longer running stability, 127
lower memory usage, 127
MediaPicker, 123–125
MyApp with, 96
.NET Aspire, 101, 102
and NuGet packages, 98
performance boosts and bug fixes,
126, 127
platform
Android, 116–119
Geolocation, 119–122
iOS and Mac Catalyst, 115, 116
WebAuthenticator, 122
platform-specific features, 95
powerful and flexible framework, 95
smoother rendering, 127
upgrading, 97
in Visual Studio, 96

workload, 98
XAML, 99–101
.NET's future
    advancements, 207
    AI assistants, 222
    API design, 218
    Blazor, 220
    community contributions, 209
    community input shapes, 209
    cross-platform compatibility, 208
    curiosity and adaptability, 224
    innovation wave, 208
    memory and garbage collection, 215
    multi-architecture support, 217
    software development industry, 207
    tools, 208
    tuning options, 214
NoSQL database design, 166
NuGet packages, 98, 192, 196
Null-conditional assignment, 23, 24, 35
Null-conditional operators, 23, 35

O

Object-oriented language, 11
OpenAPI, 43, 44
    JSON Schema, 44
    .NET 10, 43
    NSwag, 46
    nullable types, 44
    OpenAPI document, 44
    YAML, 44
OpenAPI (Swagger) document, 47
Open-source, 9, 209, 210
OpenTelemetry, 103, 156
    specification, 180
    support, 217
Optimizations, 131–156, 191

P

Partial constructors, 32–33, 36
Partial event, 31–34
Performance-critical code, 135, 139
Performance improvements, 3, 95, 133, 157, 169, 210
Performance matters
    hardware, 131
    memory, 131
Platform's proactive approach, 216
Popovers, 115, 128, 219
Project files, 191, 195

Q

Quality tools, 200, 201
QuickGrid component, 66, 92

R

Real-time features, 86
Reciprocal Rank Fusion (RRF), 164
ReconnectModal.razor, 72
Reducing abstraction, 132
Reference type arrays, 142, 143
RightJoin, 159
Route template, 48, 80
Routing, 79, 194
RowClass parameter, 66, 92
    dynamic row styling, 66
    status, 67
RRF, *see* Reciprocal Rank Fusion (RRF)
Runtime metrics, 63–65, 155, 156

S

ScaleToAsync, 113
SDK-style project file format, 193

SDK-style projects, 189, 191, 204

SearchBar and Switch, 108, 109, 128

Security, 83, 189, 194, 215–216

Serialization, 76, 79, 140, 180, 197

Server-Sent Events (SSEs), 86, 88

    clients, 88

    HTTP, 88

Service discovery, 101–103, 217, 219

shebang (#!), 18, 19

Side-by-side testing, 200, 202

SignalR, 9, 88, 89, 93

Sorting version numbers, 175

Source control systems, 203

Source incompatibility, 187–188

Span<T> and ReadOnlySpan<T>, 29–31

Span to ReadOnlySpan, 30

SSEs, *see* Server-Sent Events (SSEs)

SSR, *see* Static server-side rendering (SSR)

Stack allocation, 139, 141, 142, 144, 178

Static extension members, 19, 35

Static server-side rendering (SSR), 82

string property, 21

String normalization, 174–175

StringSyntax attribute, 49

String to ReadOnlySpan<char>, 30

T

TableView, 109–112, 128

Target Framework Moniker (TFM), 191

TaskDto schema, 45

Task management, 39, 40, 44, 50, 54, 56

Telemetry, 101–103, 156, 179–180, 217–218

TFM, *see* Target Framework
      Moniker (TFM)

Thread pool, 148, 149, 155

    metrics, 150

    parameters, 149

TimePicker, 125, 126

TimeSpan.FromMilliseconds, 176

Traditional JIT, 212

TranslateToAsync, 113

U

Unbound generic types, 24–26, 35

V

Validation, 20, 50–53, 200

Visual Studio Code (VS Code), 48, 60,
      80, 96, 221

Visual Studio Diagnostic
      Tools, 149, 201

Visual Studio Performance, 201

W

WCF, *see* Windows
      Communication
      Foundation (WCF)

Web and native content, 108

Web application performance, 61

WebAssembly technology, 60

WebAuthenticator, 122

Web development, 2, 39, 59

Windows Authentication, 83, 215

Windows Communication Foundation
      (WCF), 190

Windows containers, 198

Windows desktop application, 208

Windows desktop technologies, 184

Windows Presentation Foundation (WPF),
      7, 8, 184

WPF, *see* Windows Presentation
      Foundation (WPF)

X

Xamarin.Forms, 95
XAML
   cleaner files, 100
   features, 100, 101
   global and implicit XML
      namespaces, 99, 100

Y

YAML output, 47

Z

ZipArchive, 177

MIX
Papier aus verantwortungsvollen Quellen
Paper from responsible sources
FSC® C105338

www.fsc.org

If you have any concerns about our products,
you can contact us on
ProductSafety@springernature.com

In case Publisher is established outside the EU,
the EU authorized representative is:
**Springer Nature Customer Service Center GmbH
Europaplatz 3, 69115 Heidelberg, Germany**

Printed by Libri Plureos GmbH
in Hamburg, Germany